FREE
═on the═
INSIDE

AAGRAPEVINE,Inc.

New York, New York

WWW.AAGRAPEVINE.ORG

BOOKS PUBLISHED BY AA GRAPEVINE, INC.

The Language of the Heart (& eBook)
The Best of the Grapevine Volumes I, II, III
The Best of Bill (& eBook)
Thank You for Sharing
Spiritual Awakenings (& eBook)
I Am Responsible: The Hand of AA
The Home Group: Heartbeat of AA (& eBook)
Emotional Sobriety—The Next Frontier (& eBook)
Spiritual Awakenings II (& eBook)
In Our Own Words: Stories of Young AAs in Recovery (& eBook)
Beginners' Book (& eBook)
Voices of Long-Term Sobriety (& eBook)
A Rabbit Walks Into A Bar
Step by Step—Real AAs, Real Recovery (& eBook)
Emotional Sobriety II—The Next Frontier (& eBook)
Young & Sober (& eBook)
Into Action (& eBook)
Happy, Joyous & Free (& eBook)
One on One (& eBook)
No Matter What (& eBook)
Grapevine Daily Quote Book (& eBook)
Sober & Out (& eBook)
Forming True Partnerships (& eBook)
Our Twelve Traditions (& eBook)
Making Amends (& eBook)
Voices of Women in AA (& eBook)
AA in the Military (& eBook)
One Big Tent (& eBook)
Take Me to Your Sponsor (& eBook)

IN SPANISH

El lenguaje del corazón
Lo mejor de Bill (& eBook)
El grupo base: Corazón de AA
Lo mejor de La Viña
Felices, alegres y libres (& eBook)
Un día a la vez (& eBook)
Frente A Frente (& eBook)
Bajo El Mismo Techo (& eBook)

IN FRENCH

Le langage du coeur
Les meilleurs articles de Bill
Le Groupe d'attache: Le battement du coeur des AA
En tête à tête (& eBook)
Heureux, joyeux et libres (& eBook)
La sobriété émotive

FREE

=on the=

INSIDE

Stories of AA recovery
in prison

AAGRAPEVINE, Inc.

New York, New York
WWW.AAGRAPEVINE.ORG

AA Preamble

Alcoholics Anonymous is a fellowship of men and women
who share their experience, strength and hope
with each other that they may solve their common problem
and help others to recover from alcoholism.

The only requirement for membership is a desire to stop drinking.
There are no dues or fees for AA membership;
we are self-supporting through our own contributions.
AA is not allied with any sect, denomination, politics, organization
or institution; does not wish to engage in any controversy,
neither endorses nor opposes any causes.

Our primary purpose is to stay sober
and help other alcoholics to achieve sobriety.

© AA Grapevine, Inc.

Contents

CHAPTER ONE

The Way Out

Finding AA in prison

CHAPTER TWO

Staying Sober In Prison

AA has many tools members on the inside can use

CHAPTER THREE

Women Helping One Another

Growing into sobriety and giving it back

CHAPTER FOUR

Walking the Walk

Using AA's Twelve Steps to grow in sobriety

CHAPTER FIVE

Sponsorship in Prison

Helping each other stay sober and learn to live

CHAPTER SIX

Carrying the Message

Outside AA members go behind the walls to share their experience and hope

Welcome

"I am currently locked up..."

Every year, many of the stories and letters received at Grapevine start in just this way. Often, they go on to detail difficult circumstances and personal histories filled with challenges. But sooner or later, there comes a change. Maybe it's the mention of a chance encounter in the prison yard with an AA member, or picking up a Grapevine magazine in the prison library or overhearing a conversation in the mess hall focused on the Big Book. The stories in this collection contain many such moments—bright moments in what can be an overwhelming sea of pain. And once AA enters the picture, with the hope it can bring to the suffering alcoholic, the stories and letters—and those writing them—begin to change, to open up. This book is a collection of such hope, including chapters about alcoholics finding AA in prison, doing corrections service, sponsoring one another and working the Twelve Steps. There's also a chapter devoted to incarcerated women.

AA members can be found anywhere, but since the early days of the Fellowship, a special emphasis has been placed on carrying the AA message to alcoholics in prison. In many places, prison groups have flourished and grown. Sadly, in others they have not. But as expressed by more than just a few of the AA members whose stories appear in this book, there are other tools that can help, such as the Corrections Correspondence Service facilitated by AA's General Service Office. Writing letters back and forth with sober members on the outside has provided a means to recovery for countless incarcerated alcoholics across the United States and Canada and, in fact, around the world. As AA's cofounder Bill W. wrote, there is something special about the communication of one alcoholic to another—something that can change lives and open up new realities:

> *"Because of our kinship in suffering, and because our common means of deliverance are effective for ourselves only when constantly carried to others, our channels of contact have always been charged with the language of the heart."*

This collection of stories from Grapevine—by members both inside and out of prison walls—is written in just that language, the language of the heart.

The Way Out

Finding AA in prison

"I remember walking around at night, screaming to the sky, 'Why can't I be like other people?'"—and that was before Jim H., whose story starts off this chapter, even went to prison. "I was sentenced to serve between 30 and 40 years. All because I couldn't stop getting loaded," he says.

But like the other members sharing their stories in this chapter, something happened to Jim, something unexpected, something wonderful. Drawn by the example of some sober AA members as they walked through the prison yard, he noticed that they were "freer in that prison than I had ever been in my life," and when he was finally released—and "went right back to my old tricks," he remembered those sober members and thought, Maybe I should call those AA people. What did I have to lose?

AA is a program of attraction, not promotion, and often, without even knowing it, AA can take hold. One member in this chapter followed a box of donuts to his first meeting in prison. Another followed the smell of the coffee. Liz B., in the story "Prison Clothes, a Meeting List and a Lot of Fear," went to the meetings just to get out of her cell. But once in the meetings things began to change. Michael T., in "The Sweet Smell of Coffee," writes, "When I sit in my group here and look around the room, I see guys from every conceivable walk of life. When I listen to other members share their stories, I feel something deep down inside myself."

Finding AA in prison is a gift many AA members in this chapter didn't expect. But once they found it, life began to open up—even behind the walls. "I truly didn't realize until I got sober that I was already living in a 'prison' on the inside, shackled and bound, suffocating with guilt and shame." So writes Cynthia P. in "This Storm Too Shall Pass." And as Elias L. shares in "Learning to Love," "It took a reckless lifestyle and 30 years of incarceration to bring me to my senses."

Freedom Is Sweet

July 2018

I grew up in a small town in Georgia. As a child, I thought the whole world drank. My folks drank and everyone we knew did.

I can't tell you when I first started drinking, but they tell me I was in diapers. My ma used to give me a shot of liquor when I was a baby. I can't remember a time when I wasn't drinking. I stole from the liquor cabinet and the fridge and finished unfinished drinks after the adults passed out. I sometimes broke into houses just to get something to drink.

By the time I was 12, and through my teens, my goal in life was to stay loaded. I got more than 20 felonies as a juvenile. I spent a lot of time in juvenile detention, boys' homes and the like.

My poor family tried to help but I wouldn't listen to them or anyone else. I was living on the streets between arrests. I remember walking around at night, screaming to the sky, "Why can't I be like other people?" I knew that if I could just act right, I could go home, where I would be able to eat good meals. But I couldn't.

I got married at 17, thinking that would automatically change me and I would become responsible. Well, we all know how that goes. I wasn't responsible enough to keep a hamster fed. I hated my weakness and inability to stop drinking. I literally used to spit at my own face when I looked in the mirror.

That same year, I went to juvenile prison. While I was doing time, my marriage ended. When I got out, I went on a rampage of armed robberies with my newfound convict friends. Of course, we were caught. I was now 18, which meant I was considered an adult in the state of Georgia. I was sentenced to serve between 30 and 45 years. All because I couldn't stop getting loaded.

I stayed drunk in prison as much as possible and was arrested all the time—in prison—for all the same things I got arrested for on the outside.

They had AA meetings where I was held, but I was way too bad and cool to attend. I had what the Big Book calls "contempt prior to investigation." But a funny thing happened as I watched those AA guys in prison. I couldn't find anything wrong with them. In fact, I was totally impressed. First, they stayed out of trouble and were released when they were supposed to be released. Also, when they walked through the prison yard—which was a jungle—you'd think they were walking through Central Park. They were freer in that prison than I had ever been in my life.

Altogether, I was locked up almost 17 years. Yet when I was finally released, I went right back to my old tricks. Finally, on March 18, 1990, I woke up on a floor filled with liquor bottles. I felt like I could not take one more step in my skin. I was done. I remembered those AA dudes in prison and I thought, Maybe I should call those AA people. What did I have to lose? So that's what I did.

It seems hard to believe, but I haven't been loaded in any way, shape or form since that day. What I found at last in AA was a solution to my problem. The Steps changed my life. In fact, I had no trouble with the First Step at all. I had been aware of my powerlessness since I was a teenager.

The wonderful people in AA made me feel like a human being for the first time in a very long time. Where I came from, nothing was free. The dessert on my tray, even cigarettes, were not free. But in AA, people gave me their time and their love and hope and wanted nothing in return. I could hardly believe it. They were for real, just like those AA guys in the penitentiary who never said a word to me but by their actions, showed me the way out. They saved my life and they don't even know.

I didn't believe in God at first. I didn't believe in anything good, really. But I stayed sober from hanging out in the rooms and working the Steps and I know I am sober today by the grace of God.

In sobriety, I've been able to be a son to my parents. All they ever wanted from me was my trust, and now I can give them that. I am an employed member of society and a lucky guy in a relationship with a beautiful AA girl. Some days I am so happy, I just want to run down the street shouting, "Life is good!"

I now take AA meetings into the jails and prisons in my area. Yeah, God has a sense of humor. I'm here to say, freedom is sweet.

Jim H.
Zephyr Hills, Florida

This Storm Too Shall Pass

Online Exclusive
October 2018

I t was the early summer of 1979 when I made the impetuous decision to pick up my first drink. I recall that day quite distinctively because the "perfect little world" that I had been living in was intensely shattered by the voices of both parents screaming the "D" world: divorce. I felt as if my heart had been broken into a million pieces. For the first time in my life, I was completely lost within myself. My sense of who I thought I was no longer existed. So I attempted to become invincible to the human race at the young age of 13.

From that day on, I don't ever remember feeling quite comfortable in my own skin. I pretended to be someone that I was not so that people would like me, but on the inside I was a "wrecking ball" and desperately seeking a way to cope. The neighborhood kids suggested alcohol to kill the gut-wrenching emotions that were tangled up inside me, so I drank to get drunk for the very first time. This was not only my first drink, but also my very first blackout.

The pattern continued throughout my teenage years, leading to my first encounter with the city police department. At 18, I was arrested for underage drinking. There were many drinking-related arrests to follow, included drinking on private property, DWIs, driving while license revoked and obstructing and delaying a public officer. The impulsive choices that I had made throughout my life led to a 58-month prison sentence. I asked myself over and over again: "Why me God? How could this happen to me?"

My freedom was suddenly stripped away and before I could catch my breath I was quickly labeled property of the state. I became just a number, isolated from the world. I truly didn't realize until I got sober that I was already living in a "prison" on the inside, shackled and bound, suffocating with guilt and shame. Today I am so grateful for the judge who recognized the dark empty hole that was in my soul as he sentenced me to two years and four months consecutive, with the condition that I receive treatment at one of the Department of Correction facilities. He said that he had a sister who had passed away from alcoholism at the young age of 29 and he was dedicated to helping me with court-ordered treatment. This was a brand-new beginning to an absolute catastrophic ending.

So it wasn't until 2008 that I was forced to come face to face with this disease through the North Carolina Department of Corrections. It was there that I attended my first AA meeting and heard a recovering alcoholic share her story. She was serving a minimum sentence of 5 years for death by motor vehicle involving DWI. As I empathized with this lady, tears began to stream down my face. All I could hear in my thoughts was: That could be me if I don't stop drinking. I came to realize that I had been a very sick individual for a long period of time and was tired of fighting a losing battle. I wrote to the on-site social workers and asked for help and from there I was sent to an intensive rehabilitation center through the Department of Corrections.

On the morning that I was transported from the prison unit to the rehabilitation center, the driver kindly whispered, "Cynthia, this is the first day of your brand-new life because you are no longer considered an inmate but a patient." I felt as if the world had been lifted from my shoulders, because finally someone recognized my incarceration was a direct result of a disease that no one wanted to suffer from. So I closed my eyes with a soft-spoken prayer and made a promise to God that I would never pick up another drink or drug again if he would just help me through the next year in this recovery process.

My new journey continued with AA meetings that were brought in to us by a home group named "Second Chances." It was at these meetings that I picked up my first white chip along with a Grapevine magazine that was literally dropped in my lap. As I began to read the stories inside its pages, I immediately found a connection with others who were out there riding the waves of this perfect storm of alcoholism. What a great feeling to know that I was not alone and that there was hope for me—but only if I became willing!

The treatment program taught me that my mind and body were physically allergic to the alcohol/drugs and that I may have been genetically predisposed at conception. The substances that I used were just mere symptoms of the underlying condition that existed inside of me. Without any hesitation, I grasped their theory and ran with it. I was finally getting the answers that I so desperately needed. The solution came easily enough—complete abstinence from all alcohol and drugs. Before I left the treatment facility, I knew that I had a question to ask myself: Do I want to live or die today?

The answer came in the realization that, for the first time in my life, I loved myself.

Early in my recovery, I blamed my parents for my alcoholism, until one day I was able to understand that both my parents were adult children of alcoholics, meaning one or both parents suffered from the disease (in this case, both grandfathers). My parents raised me the best way they knew how; it was just in my DNA that I too would succumb to this malady. (By the way my loving parents decided to stay together and have been happily married for 54 years!)

The key that opened many doors in my recovery was finding humility within all my surroundings. It didn't matter if I was sitting in the county jail missing my family or scrubbing pots and pans in the women's prison kitchen. I had to humble myself and thank my Higher Power every day for taking me away from the alcohol that nearly killed me or someone else. I soon found myself getting on my knees each night and praying to God and asking him to remove the obsession for alcohol. Then one morning I awoke and the miracle happened—it was gone.

It has been eight and a half years since I picked up a drink and I can honestly say that if it had not been for the AA groups and contacts, Grapevine, family, law enforcement and counselors while in prison, I would not be writing this article at all. Today I volunteer with the local AA group at the Women's Detention Center in the small town I grew up in, sharing my experience, strength and hope with others, hoping that one day someone will hear my message and relate to my story. For I have been given a gift above all gifts. In order to receive it, I must give it away.

Please never give up before the miracle happens, for one day this storm too shall pass.

Cynthia P.
Graham, North Carolina

Follow the Donuts

July 2016

I started drinking when I was 14. I enjoyed the feeling it gave me and found in the bottle the acceptance I wanted so badly. Alcohol helped me keep all my deeply ingrained negative thoughts buried. My life was bearable when I drank. I had found a way to cope. Sure, I did the basic things like going to school, but I stopped playing sports. I stopped doing all the things a normal 14-year-old would do and started gangbanging. I excelled at it.

My homies became the family I never had. I lived a reckless life and was accepted. I sought guidance from the older homies; they became my father figures. I wanted what they had and I got it all: the money, the property and the prestige. I looked great on the outside, but I was a wreck on the inside. Only alcohol could quiet my dark thoughts.

In 1990, at the age of 19, I was arrested and sentenced to 20 years in federal prison. The next half of my life would be spent there. I was an angry and bitter young man. I was transferred to 13 different federal prisons throughout the United States. I was kicked out of 10 of them. Now, how does someone get kicked out of a prison? I was self-will run riot. My life was unmanageable, even in the judicial system.

My alcoholism progressed while I was incarcerated; I was powerless and did not even know it. I found myself constantly being placed in a special housing unit for being drunk, which I always denied. Alcohol was a vehicle for escaping the reality of being in prison because it kept me in a fog. The world was against me, God had betrayed me, just as my co-defendants had, and I felt that I wasn't responsible for the way my life had turned out. I thought God hated me.

Fifteen and a half years passed in the blink of an eye. I was now a 35-year-old man with the spiritual mentality of a 19-year-old. On July 2, 2005, just after the 4:00 o'clock count, I was sitting in the day room just as I had done for years—drunk and nodding out. But for some reason, that day was different. I could hear everybody laughing and saying, "Man he's been like that ever since I've known him." I heard it as clear as day, but I couldn't respond. Those words hurt because it was true.

That night I woke up scared. I had 10 months left on my sentence and I realized I hadn't accomplished anything in my life. I called out, "God, if you're real, please help me. I can't go home like this, and I don't know what to do. Please show me what to do. I want to stop drinking. Show me what I must do."

The next morning, I woke up and felt an urge to be quiet and still. As the housing unit was being released for the noon meal and the inmates headed to the chow hall, I went outside to smoke a cigarette. Watching the movement of the yard I saw one of the counselors escorting a group of men and women volunteers. I noticed that one of the women was carrying a pink box. I instantly knew that it contained donuts, and I hadn't had a donut in 15 and a half years. I figured that the volunteers were members of some religious group wanting to save the lost souls roaming the prison yard.

I figured if I said a couple of hallelujahs and a few amens they would offer me a pastry, so I followed them. I stood at the door and looked through the glass and when the woman motioned for me to come in I asked, "What's this?" "This is a meeting of Alcoholics Anonymous," she responded. "Oh no, I'm not an alcoholic," I said. She looked at me and smiled. Then she opened the box. "Would you like a donut?" she asked. I accepted her offer, went in and sat next to the door to enjoy my pastry.

I noticed six guys, all of different nationalities, who I would often see walking the track together. They were sitting in the room talking and laughing. I thought they had turned religious, because I would see them all on the bleachers reading a big blue book. I figured it was the Bible.

The woman began the meeting with the most profound words I had ever heard: "God grant me the serenity to accept the things I cannot change, courage to change the things I can." Those words shook me to my very core. I was compelled to stay. Then the woman spoke and told my story. She knew how I felt; she knew how lost I was. However, she also said that she had a solution and that she followed some simple suggestions, which are defined in 12 Steps.

My curiosity got the better of me and I kept going back to those meetings, looking for holes in their program—but I didn't find any. I didn't drink. I stayed sober, and kept going back. I could not believe that I was relieved of the obsession to drink each day.

I started walking the yard with those people I had met in there. I started doing things differently. My homies thought I had lost it. They thought that all the time I had done had finally gotten to me. I told them, "No, homie, I finally found it!"

I was released in November of 2006. Instead of calling my mother to pick me up, I called Alcoholics Anonymous. They came, picked me up, took me straight to a meeting and asked me to lead it. I wanted what they had; I wanted a new start on life and was willing to do the work. I had to change everything about myself. I could not hang out with the old homies anymore. I could not live in the old neighborhood. I shut up and listened. I did what I was told. I got a sponsor, did the Steps and did service.

I've had quite a life since I've been what I call "back in America." The miracles of the program do come true. After two years on probation, my probation officer called me and said, "We're wasting our time with you; you do not need to be on probation. Look at all the good things you are doing with your life." On Christmas Eve of 2008, I got the call. The judge who had given me all that time had terminated the remaining four years of my probation. I was a free man now—both inside and out!

Today I'm all about service and giving back. And guess what? I have the clearance to go into jails and carry the message of AA to people just like me. Imagine that. And you know what I tell them? I tell them, "Come as you are, but don't leave as you came. Life is not always easy, but I don't have to drink, and I don't have to live in an 8 feet by 6 feet cell ever again—and neither do you."

D.V.
Pacific Palisades, California

The Sweet Smell of Coffee

April 2020

I arrived at the maximum-security state prison at Elmira, N.Y. in 2014. As the correctional bus pulled up to the facility, I could never have imagined beyond my wildest dreams what I'd discover up on that hill.

The prison building's structure has an intimidating appearance, with a really high wall. It's got to be at least 40 feet high. Once inside the facility, I was soon greeted by an inmate who asked me if I was interested in attending AA there. I was open to the suggestion. I had been in and out of trouble and in and out of solitary confinement. My life was pretty unmanageable.

I will always remember my first AA meeting here at Elmira. I was quite nervous. The group was called The Hill Group and it was held in the facility's school building. This one was on a Wednesday night, and I was told ahead of time that there'd be outside AA members in attendance.

I had always struggled in social settings when alcohol wasn't involved. And I was an introvert. But whatever anxiety I experienced that night subsided. I received a warm welcome by everyone at the meeting. Moreover, I had the opportunity to meet at least 20 different sober prisoners who lived in various housing units throughout the complex.

What I definitely remember is the smell of coffee brewing. The room was decorated with all these AA slogans, and there was plenty of literature—tons of it. I welcomed myself to some literature. I learned about the history of The Hill Group. It's been in existence since President Kennedy was in the White House! Also, this group has saved many, many lives of inside members, as well as outside members.

During the meeting, we went around the room reading the Preamble, the Steps and some AA literature. The chairperson that night stressed the importance of anonymity and asked if there were any newcomers, so I raised my hand. Later, we had a coffee break and when the meeting ended, we gathered and said the Lord's Prayer. They told me to come back. I'm glad I did.

At one point in my life, I wanted the world and everything in it. Unfortunately, alcohol and other substances had their way with me. I came to prison for the first time at the age of 31. I now had a sentence of 30 years to life.

I truly believe that The Hill Group has made me a better person. Prison is full of negativity and temptations. Every day above water is a good day in here. I've learned that alcoholism is a disease that strikes at random; it doesn't discriminate. When I sit in my group here and look around the room, I see guys from every conceivable walk of life. When I listen to other members share their stories, I feel something deep down inside myself. I learn that other people are no better nor less than me. We're all equal in AA regardless of how much sobriety we may or may not have.

Our elections for service at The Hill Group are coming up. I've held the literature position for the past year. It was such a rewarding experience. However, I can't say that I've read all the literature yet. I will say that what I read has made me more knowledgeable about the history of AA, how it started and why it still exists today.

Before I found AA in prison, I was labeled by the administration as a disruptive inmate. Convicts who know me can attest to that. Finding this group is saving my rear each and every day. Growing up and taking responsibility for my actions, past and present, is what I do today. It's who I am. My relationships with family and friends have improved dramatically since joining AA. Now it's about working the Steps, carrying the message and improving my relationship with my Higher Power.

I started a hobby in here about a year ago, painting subjects in different mediums. A fellow member at our group was kind enough to give me some of his extra paint brushes. This took my imagination to new levels. Recently, with help from various family members, I was able to turn my cell into a little art studio. I've painted several pieces since and sent them to family and friends for the holidays. The feedback from everyone has been overwhelming. I owe that to The Hill Group.

I've been incarcerated almost 17 years now. I may never see the outside world again. I have good days and bad ones. But don't we all? I know I must continue to change.

For me, sobriety is a gift that's earned every single day, just like most people earn a living on the outside world. Each and every hour, day, month and year that I don't pick up that first drink, I earn that gift. And then I try to help another member achieve that same reward.

Michael T.
Stormville, New York

The View From My Prison Window

July 2003

According to my deceased brother, whom drug and alcohol abuse took before the age 25, I was once found passed out behind some bushes at the side of a brick home in an Atlanta suburb, with an empty can of beer at my side. I was five years old. I had stolen the beer and some toys from a neighbor's home, and was in my hideout.

Even at the age of 5, I lived a life lived with shame and guilt, which was the fuel of my disease. Later, various people predicted that I would be dead by the age of 16 or 18, or 21, at the most. I was surprised myself to see the age of 30. I am now 45, and I have been clean and sober for seven years, which is a miracle in itself, though I am a miracle. I am just evidence that this can happen.

I grew up robbing and stealing in an effort to fight off feeling restless, irritable, and discontent. My illegal proceeds went toward the purchase of a chemical fix for a spiritual problem. As a result of such actions, I have spent the majority of my life behind steel bars, concrete walls, and barbed wire fences decorated with razor wire. I am presently serving a 420-month federal sentence that I have served 14 years and three months on.

Five years ago, I was sent to the United States Penitentiary (U.S.P.) Lompoc, in Lompoc, California, against my will. It turned out to be a blessing. While there, I learned what Alcoholics Anonymous is really about—thanks to the loving members inside, several outside guests with multiple years of sobriety, and our staff sponsor, also an alcoholic, who went the extra mile to see that we had several meetings available.

I am no longer restless, irritable and discontent. Today I am OK, and have learned how to live life sober. I still have my struggles, of course, but I am able to see them as a part of God's will for my life, and I look to see what there is to be learned from them.

I have come to believe that all things happen for a reason, and that even though it may be hard to see at times, there is a spiritual lesson to be learned in all situations.

I was transferred from Lompoc to U.S.P. Pollock, in Pollock, Louisiana, in August 2001. I did not want to come here, but I have accepted it as God's will, and have done the next right thing program-wise. Many of us from Lompoc were torn away from our wonderful program there, and some of us have helped to get meetings started at other institutions, because we have learned the value of what it means to carry the message to those who suffer from the disease of alcoholism.

Today, in light of my circumstances, I am able to look out of a prison window into the sky, or above the walls (my cell is on the fourth floor), to see the beauty of God's creation. The beauty was there all along, but it was hard to see it with a soul filled with darkness. Alcoholics Anonymous helped to open my eyes and heart to let the light shine in, and for that, I am forever grateful.

Wayne D.
Pollock, Louisiana

Learning to Love
June 2020

Today, I can say, "I love AA." But it wasn't always this way.

I had my first beer at age 8 and acquired a taste for it at 10. A judge mandated me to go to AA meetings when I was 12, but he just didn't understand, I told myself. Who was he to tell me where I was going to end up if I didn't change my ways?

Later, I had a probation officer. For five years, she encouraged me to attend AA. She was even willing to sit beside me at AA meetings, but the fear of not knowing what AA would do to me kept me from attending. Would it change me? Would I still be able to hang out with my homeboys? I was more concerned about what other people thought of me than my own well-being.

Despite the blackouts I had in my teens, I defended my drinking tooth and nail. My life took a turn for the worse. I began to drink and use drugs and the combination landed me in the hospital a few times with an overdose. Soon I began breaking into cars. At times I turned to burglary to quench my need for alcohol, which increased my interactions with police. I was OK with that because I was too far gone to understand the seriousness of my actions. I was even shot and stabbed, yet I didn't see my drinking as a problem. I didn't sleep on the curb or a park bench. I had a home. I could not be an alcoholic.

My drinking began to affect my relationships with family, friends and my colleagues at work. Yet I felt indestructible. Unlike Superman, who was weakened by Kryptonite, alcohol made me stronger, or so I believed. But in reality, the more I drank, the more problems I created. I blamed the police for my arrest, the district attorney for pushing for my conviction and the judge for believing them and not me. I also blamed society for not giving me a second chance. In reality, it was I who had failed society's many opportunities for me to change my self-destructive ways.

Soon all the chaos my drinking created turned violent and I ended up killing two people. I spent the next four years in county jail fighting the death penalty.

While I sat in a cell awaiting my destiny, I learned all the tricks of how to smuggle oranges and sugar in from the chow hall to make "pruno," also known as inmate-manufactured alcohol. Pruno became a power greater than myself. I fell under its spell. It allowed me to disregard the consequences of taking two human lives. It drowned my guilt and shame for committing such horrible crimes, and yet I still couldn't admit I was an alcoholic.

Soon the parole board made me attend AA meetings. I came into AA judging and criticizing everyone who shared. I rolled my eyes when I believed people were lying. I was a harsh critic. Yet in the back of my mind, I'd recall stories and phrases from the meetings that caught my attention, and damned if it didn't seem like they were talking about me. Then one day, somehow, I came to recognize that my life was identical to theirs. Maybe I was an alcoholic after all.

As my curiosity grew, I found out about Hospitals & Institutions panels. These caught my attention, not because I knew what they were about, but because I noticed the people bringing them in weren't wearing prison uniforms.

Soon something began to happen. I no longer felt forced to attend those AA meetings. I found myself picking up coffee cups after, taking out the trash or helping to set up the room. I started doing service without even knowing it.

As I began to grasp meetings, I set out to do what people would call "working the program." Actually, I did what I believed to be working the program. I began memorizing and reciting the Steps. I thought that was all there was to working the Steps. This is easy, I told myself. Who needs a sponsor for this? So I taped a copy of the Twelve Steps under the top bunk in my cell and I kept a pocket-sized copy in my wallet. I recited the Steps everywhere I went...in the cell, walking in the recreation yard, walking to chow or at work. As far as I knew, I was working the program! I was so cocky about my understanding of the Steps that I couldn't wait for the parole commissioner to ask me about them during my hearing.

When that time came, the commissioner asked, "Do you know the Steps?" I quickly answered that I did, and he asked, "How many are there?" I told him there were 12. "Do you know Step Four?" he asked.

I looked at him and gave him a smile as big as the Joker in Batman. Then I recited Step Four loud and clear. He wasn't done though. He quickly asked, "Do you apply it to your daily life?" I didn't hesitate to answer loudly, "Yes."

Later, I bragged about this on the yard, but I got to wondering... What is Step Four and how do you apply it in your life? I realized then that the commissioner knew I was full of it. That's why he gave me a five-year parole denial.

After that, I got the courage to write to the General Service Office using the address in the back of the Big Book. I asked for a sponsor and they sent me information on how to get one. Eventually, I got a letter from a recovering alcoholic agreeing to sponsor me through the mail. His patient guidance and understanding led me to slowly gain a much better understanding of the AA program.

As I continued to work with my sponsor, my understanding expanded, and this led me to reestablish a relationship with a Higher Power. My eyes and mind opened up. I came to recognize where and when I had closed the door on my Higher Power as a teenager. Today, the relationship that I have with my Higher Power is one that allows me to see how he works in my life, strengthening my faith and giving me hope that this cell won't become my casket.

Over time, as I continued to grow in the program, my life changed. I learned to smile and greet strangers. I began to feel love and care for other people. It took a reckless lifestyle and 30 years of incarceration to bring me to my senses.

My Higher Power finally released me from jail and put me back home to be with my 88-year-old mother, my brothers and sister and the daughter I left behind when she was 5. He also gave me the opportunity to establish relationships with people I had not known would be part of my life, my beautiful granddaughters, nieces and nephews.

Most importantly, AA has given me the opportunity to make amends to my victims, my victims' families and to the community I have taken so much from.

Today, I have a sobriety date of January 14, 1992. I am grateful to be 28 years sober. Without AA, I ran my life ragged, into darkness. With AA, I finally found myself surrounded with people who love me, encourage me and support my recovery. They help bring me into the light.

Elias L.
Downey, California

Prison Clothes, a Meeting List and a Lot of Fear
July 1996

My first experience of Alcoholics Anonymous meetings was in an Oklahoma state prison. I went to the meeting to get out of sitting in my cell. I wasn't really interested in the program, just in getting out of the cell. There were three people who came in from an outside group in the city to sponsor our prison AA group. It was hard for me to understand why these strange people gave up their free time to come into prison and waste it on convicts like me.

I'm not sure when the light shone on me, but I started to listen and participate in the meetings. Everyone there was telling my story. I realized I wasn't so different and so alone.

About two months before my release from prison, I started noticing that other inmates, who were released to the outside world, were returning to prison. Most of the reasons given were that they couldn't stay sober and clean out there. I knew I was getting out soon and I was afraid. I talked with a sponsor from the outside and she told me I had to go to an AA meeting as soon as I got out. She gave me a list of meetings in my home area and suggested that I make 90 meetings in 90 days.

I'll never forget that terrible, terrible day I was released. I was so scared. I didn't want to leave prison! I knew I couldn't live out there. It wasn't my world. My world was behind those tall fences with barbed wire with guards who told me what to do all the time; my world was structured by someone else. I had nothing to go home for, just the same life that had put me where I was. I just couldn't do it alone! I made a suicide plan.

I got to the town I once called home with nothing but my prison clothes, a list of AA meetings, and a lot of fear.

I remember walking up to a big house with the letters AA on the doorway, not really having any hope. No one could know how I felt. All

I could think of was this little old lady, who came into the prison every week, saying, "When you get out, go to a meeting. There is a solution." I walked in the door and I was greeted with smiles and handshakes. They asked me my name and told me their names. In the meeting I heard my story all over again. I felt welcomed and I knew I was really home, and everything would be OK for that day.

It's been years since I left prison. I finally found out why that old lady and those strange people wasted their free time. I hear it in the meetings often: You can't keep it if you don't give it away.

Liz B.
New Iberia, Louisiana

Young and Sober in Alaska
Online Exclusive
August 2013

My life took an amazing turn October 5, 2012. During the four years before that, I had been an active alcoholic and addicted to painkillers. My heavy drinking began when I was in high school. I would sit in the back row of my classes and secretly sip out of the tall boys I'd snuck in.

Although I loved to read and my childhood dream had been to become a writer, I loved being a rebel who ditched class with my friends. Obviously, I didn't take school too seriously and eventually I just stopped going.

My best friend David and I would spend most of our days together driving around in his old car drinking with the music turned up. Other days, we'd just hunker down in a park and drink the day away there.

David was the only friend I had whom I was able to confide in, laugh with and of course, drink with. Alcohol was like our mutual friend who comforted us and quieted our demons.

Sobriety never interested me; nor did life at that point. That changed when my girlfriend, Mattie gave birth to our daughter several years ago. When my little girl arrived in this world, I knew it was time to slow down on my drinking and also start earning a living.

After six exhausting months of looking for work, I found a job as a material builder working on a production line 12 hours a day, six days a week. Working that kind of schedule didn't leave me a lot of time to do much else.

At this job, I got in the habit of drinking on my lunch break. I would go to the nearest store, buy some alcohol and get as buzzed as I could before I had to return to the production line. This went on daily for many months. Around this time, I added painkillers to the mix. At times I was so hungover, I missed work. But I still thought I was in control.

One day after work, I learned from a friend that my old close friend David had committed suicide. It didn't hit me right away; it took a few days for the reality to sink in. But when it did, it was overwhelming. I felt like a blanket of exhaustion covered my whole body. I would play some sad songs over and over and get drunk and cry about it all.

After his death I drank even more and took even more painkillers. Eventually I lost my job. Unemployed, I now had more time to drink and take pills. Most of my money from unemployment went to these things. And I found myself struggling to pay my rent.

I was lying to myself. I told myself that I was getting by and everything was OK. Well, it wasn't. My unemployment ran out and because I didn't have my G.E.D., nobody wanted to hire me.

In October, I was arrested. I was placed in a cell with a man whom I will call Brother Rick. He reminded me a bit of my dad. He invited me to go to an AA meeting and although I didn't believe I had a serious problem, I went along. That first meeting opened my eyes to everything.

I realized the severity of my problems. At this point, I was 25 years old and I didn't really know where the last several years had gone.

I've been sober since the day after my arrest. I've stayed sober while in jail—which can be quite a challenge.

I've gotten my head so straight now that I can write again, love again and see again.

AA saved my life when Brother Rick reached out to me. I will forever be grateful for that. God works in such mysterious ways. I know that I will never have to go through this sobriety journey alone. It feels good to be young and sober!

John H.
Anchorage, Alaska

The Birdsong in Prison
July 2011

I have served 38 months of a 40-month prison sentence. Thirty-six of those months have been spent in AA. I've had two different sponsors, and I was guided through the Steps with each one. I've been active in service and have had the pleasure to sponsor another inmate.

Each time I go to a meeting, I go with an attitude that I must listen, and with an expectation that I'll hear something that's going to help me in my sobriety.

Last week, the speaker was sharing his experience, strength and hope, and as I was listening I became distracted by the loud chirping of some birds outside of the window.

Fearing that I might miss hearing something important, I began to use every ounce of mental energy I could to ignore the loud chirping and listen to the speaker, but to no avail. My mind was hypnotized by the chirping and my thoughts began to leave the meeting and travel into my past.

I thought about how prior to my arrest—or rescue—I was in active alcoholism, and ended up homeless, living in a park in New York City.

In the wee hours of each morning before the sun would rise, and before the break of daylight, the sound of birds chirping would wake me up as I lay sleeping on the park bench. I hated hearing them chirping as they proclaimed daylight's approach. Each day for me meant yet another day of pain, misery and suffering.

As I brought my thoughts from way back then to now, I realized that I am no longer sitting in a park bench, I am sitting in an AA meeting; I am no longer alone, I am surrounded by guys who care about me; I am no longer drinking, I am sober; and I am no longer filled with fear and confusion, I have peace and serenity.

Although I wasn't able to hear everything the speaker shared, I believe that my Higher Power directed me to hear exactly what he wanted me to hear—those birds chirping. It was a sound I used to dread that is now music to my ears. I left the meeting grateful. Thank you AA.

Eric O.
Wallkill, New York

2

Staying Sober in Prison

AA has many tools members on the inside can use

Not everyone who comes to AA—either in prison or on the outside—gets sober right away. For some, the pathway to sobriety is marked by stops and starts. But, like Todd K. in "Out of the Hole," outside AA members who brought meetings into the institution he got transferred into "assured me I could do this program no matter how many times I had failed."

Perseverance and a willingness to "keep coming back" is a characteristic shared in many of the stories in this chapter, and once a serious start on the program has been made, incredible results can often follow. Says Bradley W. in "Bring to the Table," "Other inmates said they'd heard of AA or had attended meetings, but most said they hadn't given AA an honest effort or hadn't been ready to work the Steps." But after giving AA a real shot himself, says Bradley, "My AA work has made prison an endurable punishment. I'm getting to know, laugh at and love the sober version of myself." And, as Ben L. shares in the story "A Bit of Cheer in a Tough Place," "AA is in the heart. It's always with me, even on days when I feel I'm in the great AA desert."

That desert can stretch a long way, and there are a lot of tools AA members on the inside use to get and stay sober—like AA Grapevine magazine, the Big Book, and staying connected with members on the outside through GSO's Corrections Correspondence Service. "Every time I felt I was at the end of my rope, I'd get a Grapevine or a letter from one of the people I'd met since I'd gotten sober," says Anthony C. in the story "In Need of a Hug." Now on the outside,

Anthony always supports efforts to provide AA literature to meetings in prison. "Big Books never go to waste," he says. "You can throw a Big Book out the window and you will always hit a drunk in the head."

Bring to the Table

July 2019

I have no control in my life. I am literally told when and what I can do, right down to when I am allowed to use the bathroom. Without acceptance, I don't see how enduring this prison—and the hourly challenges that arise—could be possible.

Before I explain these difficulties, let me first touch on the tools I was given before incarceration.

I first attended an AA meeting that was spectacularly large. I was initially brought to a "pre-meeting" with a handful of other newcomers. I endured this First Step meeting as best I could and was then shepherded to the basement of a megachurch where more than 200 people were gathered. I was terrified, but since I had not driven there, I felt like I could neither run nor hide.

I felt the blood drain from my face down to my feet, making the effort to walk forward into this gathering even more difficult. Defensive daggers were firing from my eyes. The people in that huge meeting seemed to look at me all at once. I was sure they could see right through me. I tried to box them away by fiercely glaring. But most of these alcoholics donned a smile, the kind of smile that flaunted some big secret that they weren't about to let me in on.

That didn't turn out to be true. Through many more meetings, Step work and sponsorship, I had unintentionally prepared myself for the incarceration indignities to come.

Life in prison is like reliving the worst possible high-school experience that anyone could imagine. There's a social hierarchy in prison. Everyone is watching you, everyone is gossiping about you, and no one can be trusted. Many (not all) of the correction officers are versions of high school. The level of pettiness some of them enjoy inflicting is staggering. Everything in prison—literally everything—is an uphill battle, and that battle is intentionally made more difficult and frustrating by the staff and other inmates.

I try not to pass on incorrect information to others. Truth in prison is only as reliable as one might allow for another inmate's "knowledge" or a guard's poorly disguised "guidance," which is often meant to sabotage. After all, prison isn't supposed to be fun or comfortable. Thankfully, I can accept all of this and more.

Acceptance is the answer to all my problems today, is the thought I keep in mind as I trudge through each day here. I make every effort to work on becoming a better version of myself and developing a stronger relationship with my Higher Power.

One day, something remarkable happened when I was reading my Big Book. Maybe it was God's whispered suggestion or the AA Responsibility Declaration tugging at the back of my mind. Whatever the inspiration, the next right thing to do became urgently apparent. Instead of remaining in the confines of my cell doing my AA work, I relocated to the prison "day room," the inmates' shared common space. There I sat reading, highlighting and writing in my Big Book, *Twelve Steps and Twelve Traditions* and *Daily Reflections* books.

This attracted the attention of other inmates, who wondered what I was up to. Soon my work became a conversation starter. Other inmates said they'd heard of AA or had attended meetings, but most said they hadn't given AA an honest effort or hadn't been ready to work the Steps. So I invited them to join me and decide for themselves if they wanted to see how I worked my AA program.

If prison is like a high school, the table I was doing my AA work at quickly became the most desirable lunch table in the cafeteria. Guys wanted to sit at the "in table," be a part of the AA crew and talk about alcoholism. I became immersed in remarkable discussions and stories and happily shared mine.

It took me a few months to recognize what was happening every day in our day room. We were reading AA literature together and I found myself answering a lot of questions I never thought I'd be in a position to answer. Some of the Promises began to materialize right there under my nose. The opportunity to act as a temporary sponsor to these guys soon came naturally.

What we were doing wasn't only for the prison in-crowd. Involvement in AA can be easily replicated on any of an institution's units, which is far better than leaving us to our own misery, knuckling our foreheads in anger and self-pity.

Our literature tells us that a meeting takes place when any two alcoholics get together and share their experience, strength and hope. I'm grateful for the opportunity to feel whole and a part of something so much bigger than myself. My AA work has made prison an endurable punishment. I'm getting to know, laugh at and love the sober version of myself. I can't stress the importance of self-love enough. In my inventory, self-hatred was my biggest resentment.

Alcoholic newcomers on the unit have the same skeptical and contemptuous eyes I once had. Remarkably, now I'm the one sporting that obnoxious, knowing grin. I'm one of those who know a "secret" and it is a secret I excitedly share with anyone who wants in on it. Recovery, happiness and forgiveness are possible.

AA in prison is like a kind of homework that is challenging, fun and rewarding at the same time. It makes graduating into the best version of ourselves something to be excited about sharing. And it certainly makes this time spent incarcerated worthwhile.

Bradley W.
Plymouth, Wisconsin

In Need of a Hug
December 2017

When I had 10 months sober, I went to prison. It was quite a culture shock. I had been going to AA meetings almost every day and now I was locked in a prison that had one meeting a month. We could only have a meeting when one of the staff was willing to volunteer to sponsor it.

When I was sentenced, the judge gave me time to get my affairs in order. On the positive side, I was returning to the same prison that I had been released from five years earlier. I say the "positive side" because I knew the prison's address and could have a Grapevine subscription sent to myself there. I also brought all my books with me, the Big Book, *Twelve Steps and Twelve Traditions* and *As Bill Sees It*.

Walking back into prison was a shock. An old buddy of mine was in the yard, waving to me. I had friends who were still there. Some had never left. Others, like me, had gone out and come back in.

I was scared, not of being in prison, but about whether I'd be able to stay sober in prison. I had started to become this different person through working the Steps. I wasn't sure if I could be a new person in prison.

When I was first incarcerated, there was no mention of an alcohol problem. I was classified as a career criminal, a violent offender with a parole violation and a new charge. Nowhere did it say that I was a suffering alcoholic in need of a hug.

I felt like I was losing my mind. It seemed all I could do was walk the track and pray. My entire support system had been ripped out from under me.

There was an oldtimer at my outside home group who used to say the same thing every day. The kind of one-liners that sound profound the first time you hear them, but after the hundredth time start to become annoying. As it turns out, his voice saying the same thing over and over again was all I could hear in prison. It was such a blessing. I started to calm down and had one of those "Ah ha" moments in which I realized why God had me hear his voice saying the same thing over and over.

Finally, my first Grapevine came. I wanted to run to my cell and read it cover to cover. I forced myself to read just one story a day. It was my meeting in print. It was a daily life preserver.

That's how my time went as I settled into my sentence. Every time I felt I was at the end of my rope, I'd get a Grapevine or a letter from one of the people I'd met since I'd gotten sober. I sometimes got a card that my home group passed around on holidays with words of encouragement from members I did and didn't know. Since getting out, I always sign cards when people pass them around. I learned how important they can be.

Then the day came when we had our first AA meeting. I had told my buddy I was done with the old life. I also said I was going to AA. He figured it was just a phase I was going through. He said I was only doing it to look good for the parole board. It was pretty hard walking away from my friends in the yard to go to my AA meeting.

In 1990, a friend from my old home group sent me the loner's newsletter. I wrote to the General Service Office in New York City asking to become a loner. They wrote me back and said that I was not a loner but a convict. They went on to tell me about the prison correspondence program. After getting over my resentment about their answer, I wrote and asked to have an outside member I could write to. They put me on a list of people waiting to get AA prison correspondence letters. I was kind of surprised. I thought people were always doing this type of service work.

About a month later, I got a letter from a guy in a halfway house who needed someone to write to. I thought it was a funny situation. Here I was, about a year and a half into my prison sentence, telling a guy in a halfway house about the program. When all else fails, work with another alcoholic!

Soon after, I was shipped to another prison. When you move, they take all your belongings, give you a jumpsuit and put you on a bus. We were dropped off in "holding" at another prison. I had been there before, in "population." We were locked in this holding dormitory with people from all over the country. We only got out to go to the mess hall.

It was nonstop noise. After a few days, I felt as if I were losing it. I had no books, no phone numbers and no mail. All I could do was pray. I would go to the bookshelf every day trying to find something to read. I've always been an avid reader and I could lose myself in a good book. The problem was that the books in holding were the ones no one wanted. After about a week, I looked at those unwanted books again. Out of the corner of my eye, I saw what looked like a Big Book. I kind of casually walked over and took it off the shelf. Sure enough, it was a Big Book!

I went back to my bunk clutching the book like a life preserver. As I opened it, I noticed the inside cover was signed. It had been sent to an inmate from a group on the West Coast in 1978. Now, I was holding it on the East Coast in 1990. I knew that my Higher Power had brought that book to me. I thought of all the other hands it had gone through. When I finally got shipped out, I put the book back, to pass it along for the next inmate who was going to need it.

At my home group, I always vote to bring books into the prisons. Big Books never go to waste. You can throw a Big Book out the window and you will always hit a drunk in the head.

Luckily, the final prison I lived in was very open to AA, and we had meetings every week. But it was the same handful of guys. We would get sick of telling each other the same stories, so I asked the counselor if he would be open to outside AA people coming in. He thought it was a good idea.

I wrote to AA World Services again and asked if they could contact an area group who might be interested in helping us. Within a month, we had outside members coming in. It turns out a home group in the area had approached the institution when it was built and had gotten members approved, then never heard back until World Services contacted them.

For those who are interested in taking a meeting behind the walls, it's not necessary that you ever committed a crime. If you're an alcoholic and you're now sober, you have something to share. And you don't even have to know how to swear.

Anthony C.
Fairport, New York

A Bit of Cheer In a Tough Place

December 2019

I n March of 2018, Grapevine ran my article, titled "Doin' Time With Aunt Suzy." I wrote about the immense support I got from my Aunt Suzy—who now has 27 years of AA experience and sobriety—while I was in prison.

I'm still doing time in prison, but the growth I've experienced from working the Steps and practicing the Traditions continues to make positive changes in my life.

I've learned that when I practice the principles of recovery, they tend to be contagious, especially in here where we spend time together in close quarters day in and day out. As I continue to work on my humility and honesty, I notice others practicing humility and honesty. It affects the lives of fellow inmates and the correctional officers around me. There's only one explanation: God working in the miraculous beautiful way he does.

One of the more powerful aspects of living life in prison is change. In here, it can feel so controlling and completely debilitating. A sense of sanity can come from having a cellmate you like or just from having your cell decorated and organized. But everything can change at a moment's notice. This was my experience this past September.

At 4:45 one morning, a beam from a flashlight hit me in the face as I was sleeping. I woke and jumped up. "What's going on?" I asked. "Pack it up, you're moving," a correction officer replied. I asked him how much time I had to pack and get dressed. His reply was overwhelming. "Thirty minutes," he said.

In a matter of 30 seconds, I learned I had just a half hour to pack all my belongings and say goodbye to what I called home for four years. One of the hardest parts of the 30 minutes was thinking of all the guys and outside volunteers of our AA group who I wouldn't get a chance to say thanks and goodbye to. I had worked so hard to get these three years of sobriety and to build meaningful relationships just for them to disappear in what seemed like a snap of a finger. Three hours later, I arrived at my new "temporary home" facility.

Change is tough. I am now in a treatment program for sex offenders—a label that I have for life, a direct result of my drinking and poor decisions I made when I was 19. I'm now 30. Gratefully, with the help of God, I've been able to slowly adapt to my new environment.

There is no grass in our little yard here. We're surrounded by walls; it's the complete opposite of my old facility. I really miss my guys and the AA volunteers back there: Dave B., Charles, Gloria, Dale, Jeff and Bart.

Gloria used to say, "For every mile of highway there are two miles of ditches. When I'm working the program, I'm on the highway; once the program falls to the side, so do I, straight into the ditch."

Here at this new prison I often feel like I'm in a desert: AA just doesn't exist. At first I tried to start AA meetings, but due to the higher security level it was denied by the administration. Change—it hasn't been easy. But God always surprises me, often when and where I least expect it.

I continue to work the program with a sponsor through the mail (thanks, Ryan!). And I also stay in touch with Aunt Suzy. In the unit here where I live, I use my experience in recovery and AA to show the guys that there is hope and that by growing in recovery, we can help others.

This past Christmas God worked his magic as I've never seen in prison before. I was struggling with depression and missing friends and family, which is so common in prison around the holidays. One of the inmates who I've struggled to accept suggested that we decorate our pod. At first it seemed like an impossible feat, getting 16 guys together to do something positive, when depression and sadness were affecting many of us. But God had plans.

Then one of the guys in my pod was sitting at a table making paper snowflakes, so I decided to join him. My plan was a six-foot

Christmas tree made out of tape and paper. But before I knew it, other guys started to join us and we had a tree, ornaments and stenciled letters spelling out "Happy Holidays." It was something special that took God's help to put in place.

My favorite decoration that we made was a cardboard fireplace that had a lamp and a small fan blowing red, yellow and orange strings of yarn to look as if it were a cozy little fireplace. On Christmas morning I got to pass out chocolate cookies from the canteen with handwritten notes I'd made, all of which were "from Santa." The power of anonymity is something special.

For lunch that day we received the prison special—roast beef. And for dinner, one of the guys made everyone a burrito! It turned out to be the best Christmas I've had in years. It was even better than some Christmases I'd spent with my family back during my drinking days.

Aunt Suzy once told me that "In everything that happens, God is giving either blessings or lessons." Christmas 2018 was both for me. I learned that just because other people aren't in recovery or in AA, it doesn't mean I have to treat them differently. As the Twelfth Step says, "...we tried to carry this message to alcoholics, and to practice these principles in all our affairs."

With God's help I can carry the message, practice the principles, grow as a person and help others even when AA seems so far away. I have all the literature, and as Dave B. always says about our Big Book, "This is the repair manual to my life." But I've learned that AA is in the heart. It's always with me, even on days when I feel I'm in the great AA desert. It's up to me to carry the message in here because I don't know what God has in store or who I may help along the way.

I still miss my AA crew from my old prison home, but I also know that as I approach another holiday season in this prison, God has me right where I need to be at this very moment.

Ben L.
Cañon City, Colorado

Peace in Prison
August 1949

What can AA do for prisoners? One AA member and former prison inmate writes:

"...You can understand that when I first heard of the AA program, I wasn't particularly interested. To me it was merely a way to be released from my cell for two hours.

"One afternoon after a prison AA meeting I overheard one of the inmates (a non-AA) remark to one of the AAs who was doing 20 to 40 years: 'Hell, fellow, why do you go to these meetings? You'll never leave this place alive!' Ordinarily a remark like that, taunting a man with the fate that is always ticking in his brain, would have led to a fight, or worse. The fellow's answer took me by surprise. He had about eight years of his time in. He said that the first seven years had been a living hell, then he got on the program and had been honestly trying to live and work the 12 Steps. He said, 'My time is a lot easier to do now....' He'd been doing little things for others (big to a person in there), talking to young firsttimers, and found a peace of mind in prison to a degree that I'm having trouble finding since I got out."

Anonymous

Make It Happen
June 2015

I felt deflated as I entered the female worker pod at the Jefferson County Jail. Now, only bimonthly AA meetings would be offered. I could imagine all the work I'd done as a sober woman slowly draining away. I had just found my amazing sponsor, I'd thoroughly done the Steps and I was beginning to sponsor another woman. I was starting to feel a solid foundation of sobriety that I've only found in Alcoholics Anonymous. I was fearful because when I left this facility eight months ago, I found a reason to drink. My foundation was very unsteady back then. And now I was back. This time I knew I needed more AA!

So right away I found another alcoholic and she agreed to meet with me for daily meetings. We soon attracted other members, and although my first partner dropped out, other women began to attend. I'm overjoyed when I see the relief on a new inmate's face when she notices us sitting together with our Big Books open. We conduct our meetings just as it's done "on the outside." We're currently reading the book from cover to cover and discussing it as we go. We've also focused on topics such as relapse, and we discuss each other's current concerns.

Our inmate meetings are a grace from God. I've been able and willing to share more openly and honestly with these ladies than I had in my outside home group. We are first alcoholics, but we also share many things in common that non-inmates may not understand.

I have gotten to observe denial fading from firsttimers and new inmates. I've noticed a transformation in both of the two women who faithfully attend our meetings. They each have testified to newfound confidence and strength in their faith and sobriety. I've heard comments from them like, "It's OK if I feel anxious or if I can't sleep; I know I can get through it without taking a drink."

I've also noticed that my thinking and behavior have changed. I actually find myself using the AA principles daily. When agitated I pause before reacting. I review my day each night. I pray and meditate every day. It's become a part of who I am. I ask for help now and receive it.

I am eternally grateful to the ladies of our jail meeting group. My grandsponsor made arrangements for an AA member to meet me the day I'm released—from seven hours away! That's God. I now have some new clarity and strength to do his will. I hope this letter motivates others to create their own inmate AA meetings.

Julie C.
Telluride, Colorado

The Magic of Prison AA

July 1996

First trip to federal prison this year. Twenty-four last year. Thursday meeting starts at 7 PM. Pretty good crowd, about half and half, insiders and outsiders. Open for business by 7:10 PM. Same old stuff. Over and over. Open topic as usual. Takes a while to get rolling, need to be patient. Smoke break at 7:40 PM. Welcome relief, like an oasis. New man wants to talk. Worried about what to say. Tell him it was a blessing, just try to listen. Back into the meeting now. Things are moving right along. Not everyone is going to get to talk. As usual, it stops right at the new man. He doesn't even get called on. Windy guy, like me, took all the last five minutes. Getting close to recall—that's prison talk for "we got to go." Hurry on now. Big circle starts to form. Man on my left is shaking. Halfway through, the shaking stops. We shake hands. He thanks me for being there. What more can I say? It's 8:35 PM. now. Meeting's over but no one seems to want to leave. That's the magic of prison AA.

Anonymous
Greenville, Illinois

Accepting Myself

August 2020

I am currently locked up in prison in Virginia. Recently, I was invited to attend an AA meeting in here on Monday nights. So I signed up. At first, I didn't feel like I was an alcoholic, even though I was told I have a drinking problem. I mean, I only drank five days out of the week. How could I possibly be that much of a drunk?

But there was one problem. I was what some would call "in the closet." I went to the AA meeting, but I felt out of place, so I didn't open up about it. It felt so confusing. I stated my name, but that was all.

I felt like I couldn't "come out" in prison due to the fact that I didn't want people to judge me and I didn't want to have a lot of people trying to get with me. Besides, I felt different from the homosexuals in here. I kept my distance. I didn't trust anyone.

But I kept attending that AA meeting. There were about 14 of us who met there. Then one day, after about three months, one of the members asked me why I didn't speak up in our meeting.

"I'm not comfortable here," I said. He asked me why. "I just have a hard time opening up," I replied. "And I also have trust issues." He looked at me and said, "I understand."

Not long after that, this dude shared his drinking story in our meeting. He stated his name and said that he was a recovering alcoholic. What he said next really surprised me. He said the reason he started to use alcohol and drugs was because he was uncomfortable with trying to come out as gay to others. Then he said how AA helped him get sober and how his sponsor helped him realize that the group accepted him no matter what his race, creed or sexual identity. He then said he was proud to be gay.

I was shocked. I could believe him. I knew that if I could relate to what he said then he must be able to relate to me. So I talked to him as we walked out into the yard. I asked him how he came out and if he had feared being harassed.

First, he had to stop drinking so he could see who he was, he told me. Then he surrounded himself with people who had his best interest at heart. He also said he found a sponsor and they worked the Steps together.

And then after a moment, he stopped and said, "It's OK to cry. Let me help you through this hard time." I responded with a big OK.

For the next few weeks, we met in the recreation yard. I spilled out a lot to him. But I didn't, at that time, come out as a bisexual to anyone but him. Eventually, the big day came when I told the AA group that I felt like I had been lying to them. I cried and finally told them I was bisexual and a drunk. In the following weeks, the group helped me stay sober and get more active in AA. A few months later, I became the secretary for our AA meeting. The guy who led me to accept myself is now my boyfriend.

So I want to say thanks to him and offer hope to anyone else out there who's trying to get sober and struggling with this difficult issue. You are not alone. Keep coming to meetings. "It works if you work it and won't if you don't." AA saved my life.

Robert G.
Virginia

21 Men
July 2017

We are a group of incarcerated men who continue to carry the message despite the disruptions and distractions of prison life.

One of the biggest challenges we face each day in the treatment/behavior modification program, which we are part of, is space. Nearly 200 men compete for space in the two dorms that house us and in the common area we share during treatment hours and free time.

Within this therapeutic community, AA is voluntary. In a way, this is a good thing, for in our experience AA works best for those who aren't forced to attend. After all, as our Traditions state, this is a program of attraction, not promotion. Nevertheless, a small group of us attended a Wednesday meeting that was once hanging on by a thread. After a couple of weeks, we decided to name it Wednesday Night Circle of Hope. Although there were only half a dozen of us in attendance, we knew we had something special. We all freely share, even indulging in a little double-dipping as time allows.

But each Wednesday while our meeting took place, other inmates swarmed all around us. Some were exercising during their free time, others sat in chairs right next to us having loud conversations, all unaware of what was going on within our tight-knit circle. Often men would walk up in the middle of someone sharing and try to start a conversation with one of us. There were times when certain correctional officers would hassle us, oblivious to our purpose and despite it being posted on the evening schedule.

At first, we tried to explain to the other men the importance of these meetings to our recovery, but we soon realized the futility of our actions. At the end of the day, we were in prison and the vast majority of the men around us don't really care about our purpose, nor do they want to be in the program themselves.

At any given time, there were up to 50 inmates within a short distance of us, speaking loudly, their voices echoing throughout the space. For some of us in the circle, our disease tempted us to react with anger and frustration, but we knew that wouldn't be a practice of the spiritual principles taught in the Big Book.

We also knew that bringing this up to the staff would result in a dead end. So we carried on in the midst of chaos. When things got too loud, we just brought the circle in closer and closer.

Each week we would rotate our meeting formats: Speaker, Big Book, Step, Topic and Grapevine. For the first couple of months our members would fluctuate, but our core members (our home group) remained constant. After some time, we would count eight regular members, yet week after week the distractions and disruptions continued.

We submitted suggestions to the staff to have our meetings moved to a different part of the prison, but that would have required staffing adjustments. We chalked that up as an unattainable goal. We found that we were being tested on the principles of acceptance and tolerance. On the street, for many of us, the bottle was the solution to accepting a situation or tolerating a difficult person. Here in prison, we really have no other alternative. We have to deal with difficult situations or those situations will deal with us, likely resulting in a trip to the "hole."

Our ultimate goal had always been to have an outside AA meeting brought in to us, but we understood it can be a difficult task, and the security requirements often slow the process down even further. In the meantime, we made do with what we had: our Fellowship, the Steps and each other.

As new program members were brought in, we found our meeting was growing. Soon, we had a dozen regular members in attendance. Within the walls of the prison and the confines of our program, we were recovering. Each of us shared the sentiment that this was the best hour of our week. The message of hope had infiltrated our circle and our hearts and that message was being carried to potential new members who witnessed the growth of our circle. We soon realized that our group's primary purpose, "to carry the message to the alcoholic who still suffers," was being met.

Then one night, just four months after our little meeting of six members had started, we looked around and counted 21 men around the circle! We were full of joy and grateful to be a part of something so special.

Since that night, we regularly have 15 to 20 men in attendance. I think it is safe to say that all of us have experienced the miracle that occurs when folks get together and share their fears, concerns, experience, strength and hope.

Today, the spiritual principles taught in the Big Book are more real to us than ever. Together, we are learning patience, tolerance, acceptance and willingness.

Soon our patience—and efforts—paid off. A high-ranking correctional officer caught wind of our dilemma and allowed us to hold our meetings at a time when no one else is allowed to occupy the shared common area. At last, our Higher Power answered our prayers. And now we hold three meetings a week!

For those of us who persevered and kept coming back week after week despite the madness around us, we found that we had rediscovered the desire to remain sober. If we could find that in the midst of the chaos in here, imagine how much more we could get and give when we are granted our freedom, return home to our communities and join the Fellowship of AA in an environment of serenity and peace.

Patrick M.
Wilmington, Delaware

Why AA In Prison?

March 1953

Many ask: "What good can a man get out of Alcoholics Anonymous while serving time in prison?"

AA in prison is not primarily a means of keeping us away from alcohol; the granite blocks that impound us do that. But where a block of granite may be an obstacle in the path of some men, others find they can use it as a stepping stone to elevate themselves. We find in AA that by becoming humble, we become honest. By becoming honest we lessen our emotional conflicts. By lessening our conflicts, we clear our mental channels for acceptance of the Power greater than ourselves.

We who are members of the Folsom Prison AA Fellowship are sick and tired of battering our stubborn heads against prison walls and are trying to find the answers to the causes that brought us here. The first answer we found was self, as the initial cause of our misfortunes. In AA, we are learning to correct our shortcomings and overcome the human traits of character weakness that have led us to do the things responsible for bringing us into prison. We are taking misfortune and converting it into opportunity by establishing now a strength of character for preventing a recurrence of prison. The old adage, "an ounce of prevention is worth a pound of cure," can certainly be practiced by getting a better insight into ourselves while in prison and by practicing the principles set forth in the Twelve Steps of AA in all our affairs. We are putting into action honesty, tolerance, humility, and good fellowship while we are confined, which is helping us to prepare ourselves now for our eventual social reversion. The general consensus of men in prison, who are finding a better way of life by living the AA program, is that they are finding a way to stay out of prison, not finding a way to get out from behind bars.

We find in prison AA the difference between spending a happy day and investing it.

AA in prison is like an oasis in the Sahara; it's the smile of a friend when all else seems forsaken. AA in prison is a device to shrink a man's head and expand his heart. AA in prison shows us where real happiness begins and selfishness ends. AA in prison is for all men who seek peace of mind and who have found the courage to look into themselves.

B.P.
California

The Best Tool
July 2019

I would like to share a story with you that I feel was a divine appointment from my Higher Power working through me, AA and Grapevine.

I am in prison in Florida. I am near the end of my sentence, which enables me to sign up for a work-release program. The week that I was supposed to enroll, I was randomly transferred from the prison where I was being housed.

Instead of being anxious and fearful, I decided to trust God. My AA program has taught me to trust and believe what it says in the "Acceptance" passage in the Big Book: "Nothing, absolutely nothing happens in God's world by mistake."

Because I was in transit, I had to be housed at a reception center for five days. From there, I was transferred to my new prison.

I found out the date and time of the AA meetings at this reception center and made it a priority to make it to a meeting. When I got to the meeting room, about 12 other inmates and the two outside volunteers were already there.

I noticed several issues of Grapevine sitting on the desk in front of the volunteers. Two of the issues had articles that I had written published! The first article was "Hurricane Relief" (July, 2018); and the second was "Soul Food," (August, 2018). I decided not to mention that my articles were in those two Grapevines, as I didn't want to boost my ego.

One of the volunteers started the meeting by introducing a discussion topic of "Step One and powerlessness." This was a topic that I knew all too well. I raised my hand a few times to share, but the volunteer kept on talking every time I thought he was about finished.

I began to feel anxious, so I prayed: "God, if it's meant for me to share, then so be it." That gave me the peace of mind that I needed to calm down and listen to the volunteer as he shared. I became OK with the fact that I was there to hear the message and that it's OK if I don't get to share at a meeting.

As we were leaving, I thanked the volunteers. I was the last one to walk out of the room. I ended up walking behind three newcomers as we headed toward the dorms. I heard them talking about how alcohol ruined their lives and how they had to stop drinking. As I listened to them, I knew I had to share something with these guys.

As I approached them, I saw that they had picked up copies of the Big Book and copies of Grapevine issues with the articles that I had written. I asked them if I could share something with them. When they agreed, I showed them my articles in Grapevine. I shared with them how being in prison gave me the gift of desperation, how the Steps have changed my life and how the Promises had materialized in my life, especially the Tenth Step Promise.

As we were parting ways to go to separate dorms, I encouraged them to continue to go to meetings and work the program. They thanked me, and as I walked away, I realized that I had just had a spiritual experience.

I am extremely grateful for my Higher Power, the program of AA and Grapevine. In prison it can be hard to carry the message, but I found that Grapevine is a great tool for me to share.

Justin "Gio" G.
Port St. Lucie, Florida

Out of the Hole
July 2013

In July I was sentenced to eight years for robbing a drugstore while drunk. Certainly this harsh sentence would get me sober. But it didn't. My self-pity was deep. I spent the first two years in jail drinking and using drugs. I became so loaded on a daily basis that it was apparent to everyone. I even tried to commit suicide twice in those last couple of weeks, and failed. The powers that be rolled me up from that prison on drug charges. I went to the prison's prison—the hole. There, I came to know the loneliness that the Big Book speaks of. I was completely empty on the inside; I had nothing left. I was miserable with the drink and without.

On July 24, 2004, I asked God to help me change. That was my only prayer. I had been in and out of AA for 25 years. I knew about the program, but I never completely surrendered to it, nor to God. That day is my sobriety date.

After a rough year of getting transferred around, I ended up at a decent yard and started going to AA meetings again. I stayed sober that first year out of desperation, and by the grace of God. I made my first-ever one year without a drink in that yard. Soon I was elected chairman of our meeting, a commitment I held for the next four years.

All this was great and amazing, but I was scared to death. I was going to go home in a few years, and I had no clue how to live or function on the outside, sober. I had never done it. I started working the Steps in desperation. The H & I AA members who brought meetings in to us assured me I could do this program no matter how many times I had failed.

Somewhere between my second and third year sober, I was walking back to my cell after a meeting, and for the first time ever I felt good about my life and myself. I had true hope in that moment. It blew me away. This was a true spiritual experience. I started thanking God for everything—even the bad food and cold showers. But especially for the gift of sobriety.

Soon it came time for parole. I followed all the suggestions of my sponsor and the H & I panel members. I went to an AA meeting my first day out. I got a home group right away. I got a new sponsor, and I got into service. I have three H & I commitments now. And even though the economy is in terrible shape, I found work. And I've also since been let go. But nothing is worth drinking over today. By the grace of God and the Fellowship of AA, I have hope today. One day at a time, I don't have to drink.

Todd K.
Lompoc, California

22 Hours a Day

September 2020

'm coming up on a year of complete sobriety. I am also currently incarcerated, due to a parole violation for drinking. Since March, the three AA meetings that volunteers brought into our facility were cancelled due to the COVID-19 virus. That was bad, but it got worse. We then went into complete lockdown at the start of April.

Thank you for my Grapevines. They're the closest thing I have to AA meetings right now. They help me maintain my emotional sobriety, despite how frustrating it is being locked in my cell 22 hours a day.

When I'm frustrated, I read the "Acceptance" passage in the Big Book, the Serenity Prayer, and then I read the stories in my Grapevine. That's my AA meeting. Together they keep me calm in here. Grapevine helps remind me that taking a drink won't make anything better, and that if I do pick up (and believe me, there's booze and other things available in here), then tomorrow I either have to get sober again from scratch or get drunk again. Neither option is appealing. I reach for my Grapevine rather than the hootch, so I can put together another day sober and be OK with being in here.

Just because I'm doing time doesn't mean that I'm wasting time. I can't wait to celebrate an entire year sober.

Jude M.
Springfield, Vermont

A Twig in the Yard
July 2001

Bill M. sent us the following note along with a letter from his son, who is serving time in Kernersville, North Carolina.

This is a story about gratitude—gratitude in an unlikely setting. My son is halfway through a long prison sentence, the beginning of which marked a deep bottom in his life and the beginning of his recovery from alcoholism. He now serves as a peer counselor in a state-run program that struggles to make sobriety available in the prison environment. His growth and his Twelfth Step work constantly amaze me. A recent letter was so striking that I asked his permission to share it with you and your readers. It began with the news that he had finally been able to see a dentist—no small feat when it requires that he be transported a hundred miles to a prison facility that had such resources.

> *Dear Dad,*
>
> *Yesterday at 4:00 A.M. I was awakened in order to be taken to the dentist. It was the first time in a year that I'd been outside for a ride, so I was really excited. Of course, I had to be handcuffed to a waist chain, then shackled before*

I could get in the van. The van was brand-new: the smell was delicious and the seat was so comfortable. I must have looked like a dog out for a drive, staring eagerly from side to side. It was amazing to be moving—and in such comfort.

When we got to the facility, they took off my chains and let me walk around the prison yard. I got to touch a tree for the first time in over three years! It was an oak tree, and the bark felt so good beneath my hand. I looked up through the branches and leaves to the sun shining through. The ground was littered with small twigs and real acorns that crunched beneath my feet. The trunk, which must have been seven or eight feet around, was covered with moss and lichens. I have never seen a more beautiful sight.

As if that were not enough, a calico cat suddenly rubbed up against my leg and gave me permission to pet him while he drank from a water dish. I was dumbstruck with all the sensation. The feel of bark and cat fur, the sight of open space and green leaves—all this for a man who'd had none of them for years—were for me what climbing Mt. Everest must be to a free man. Then it ended. We left after my visit to the dentist, yet I will always carry that day with me as a symbol of God's grace and as a reminder to have gratitude for the small, mundane things of everyday life.

A twig in the yard—what joy! I'm so glad to have you to share it with. I don't think anyone else would understand.

Your son

3

Women Helping One Another

Growing into sobriety and giving it back

One alcoholic helping another is at the heart of the AA program, and it can happen in prison just as easily as it can happen outside. For the women in this chapter, after years of drinking and denial, hope appeared on the horizon in the form of AA meetings on the inside. In the story "From Chalkboard to Shackles," Sarah N. shares how powerless she was over her drinking, saying "When doctors told me if I drank again, I would die, I was drunk again within a week." Finding a meeting at the state prison for women proved to be the way out she was looking for. "Because those women were there and opened the chow hall doors each week for an AA meeting, I stayed sober, got a sponsor and worked the Steps."

Giving back what we've received is a fundamental part of the AA program and many of the women in this chapter found a way to share their sobriety and the lessons they learned with others on the inside. And it isn't just those on the inside who provide help and guidance toward sobriety and emotional growth. The outside members who carry the message into prisons are a source of gratitude. A.W. shares in her story "Nurse in Denial," "I'm so grateful for finding AA in prison and for the volunteers who brought those meetings in to us. They helped save my life, and taught me to trust my Higher Power, get honest and grow up." And an anonymous writer shares in "A Letter from Prison," "The men and women of AA who take the time out of their lives to bring us meetings are an inspiration. They give me hope for the future."

Once outside, many AAs who found the program in prison are able to carry the message back inside. Like Jamie M., in "Keeping It Real." "I couldn't wait to get off probation and go back and take AA meetings into that jail. Two years later it finally happened, and I haven't stopped since."

From Chalkboard to Shackles
March 2017

"**Y**ou are hereby sentenced to sixteen months in the California State Penitentiary for Women for two counts of felony driving under the influence of alcohol." As the judge read my sentence, my knees were trembling and my tears gushed out a flood of emotions, emotions I could no longer drown with alcohol. Just a few years prior to this moment, I stood in front of the chalkboard in my middle school classroom as a respected and admired teacher, mother and wife. Now I stood in front of the judge a shackled convict, alone, separated and spiritually bankrupt.

In college, I could drink on weekends and enjoy the occasional glass of wine, but in my mid-20s that all turned on me. I began sneaking alcohol and lying to my husband. Nearly every time I drank, I immediately went into a blackout. I did go to some AA meetings, but I was generally buzzed and never honest with a sponsor. I saw only the differences between other members of AA and myself. Over the next five years, I accumulated five DUIs. My husband ultimately divorced me and got custody of our children and I lost my teaching job and my home. All of the differences I saw when I walked into the rooms of AA became my reality. My family attempted an intervention and I wanted nothing to do with it. I didn't want to feel, so I drowned my emotions in large quantities of booze. When doctors told me if I drank again I would die, I was drunk again within a week. Perhaps prison was the only thing that could save a drunk like me.

I arrived at Valley State Prison for Women in Chowchilla, California, and was immediately introduced to "hooch" (alcohol that is brewed illegally in inmates' cells). This was my turning point. I asked myself, Am I going to drink and continue doing what I have always done or am I going to use this time in custody to better myself? I didn't drink. That same day I was walking the yard and I saw a group of women lined up at the chow hall. It wasn't chow time, so I asked another inmate what was going on and she told me, "I don't know. Some 12-step meeting." I walked through those chow hall doors and was greeted by fellow inmates with hugs, respect and understanding. Those doors were that of an Alcoholics Anonymous meeting, where I felt safe and had this strange sense that God was with me and doing for me what I could not do for myself.

I attended that A-Yard AA meeting faithfully. The women who shared their stories have had an enormous impact on my life. It is only by the grace of God that I never killed or injured anyone while I drank and drove. Some women were not so fortunate, yet they were not sulking in self-pity. Instead, they worked the 12 Steps, made amends to their victims and dedicated their lives to spreading the message of Alcoholics Anonymous on the inside of those prison walls. Because those women were there and opened the chow hall doors each week for an AA meeting, I stayed sober, got a sponsor, and worked the Steps. When those floods of emotions came (and they did and still do) I could simply say, This too shall pass. During my incarceration, I received letters from members of AA in my hometown. They sent AA literature and even helped me start another AA meeting on A-yard. Ironically for the first time in my life I felt free.

Yes, I was free in prison.

On May 2, 2012, I was released and the first place I went outside of those prison walls was to a meeting of Alcoholics Anonymous. As I write this, it is a gorgeous winter day in Humboldt County. Life keeps getting better, one day at a time. I am now a counselor at a rehab serving clients being released from prison. I am of service to AA, I have a connection with my Higher Power that keeps me sane and sober, and my daughters and I have an amazing relationship. One day at a time I am living spiritually and never forgetting the women of A-yard at the Valley State Prison for Women who helped me get through my incarceration sober.

Today I look back at my sentencing day. The true meaning of those tears I shed was that I did not have to hide or lie any more. I like to think that I am unique, that my story is more dramatic and painful than yours. But the reality is, I am just another alcoholic who needs both the Fellowship and the program of AA in order to survive one day at a time.

Sarah N.
Eureka, California

Nurse In Denial

June 2020

I grew up in a great family, with no history of anyone getting in trouble with the law or going to jail or prison. That history changed when alcohol took over my life.

My drinking began to get bad when I started my second year of college, where I was studying to be a nurse. I was your average college student who would party on weekends. After a while, I would not remember what happened over the weekend.

Over time, my drinking evolved into a couple of nights a week and then every night. Soon I found myself drinking alone in my room and hiding it from my family and friends. Surprisingly, I was able to complete college and graduate with a nursing degree.

I began my career as a nurse and moved out of my parents' home into my own house. This is when things got even worse. My drinking seemed to have taken on a mind of its own. I would work the night shift and, on my way home, I'd stop to buy alcohol. I'd make up excuses for myself to explain why I was buying something to drink at 6:00 in the morning. I just got off work, I'd tell myself. I deserve to unwind with a drink, like normal people who have day jobs.

What I didn't know at the time was that my drinking was not normal. I was a nurse. I knew what an alcoholic looked like and what they did and I was certain that that was not me. I was in complete denial.

Then one morning, something happened that changed the course of my life. I got behind the wheel of my car in a blackout and crossed the centerline and hit an oncoming car head-on. The passengers in the other car sustained minor and severe injuries. I sustained life-threatening injuries requiring numerous surgeries and months of recovery. You might think that experience would be an eye-opener for me, that I would have realized I had a serious problem. I did not.

After recovering and returning to work, I continued to drink. I was in the pure insanity of the disease. Eight months after my accident, a letter arrived from the Nursing Board stating that I was being investigated for two felonies. I spoke to the Nursing Board, and the people there confirmed that the allegations were related to the car wreck. They told me I needed to hire an attorney. I'd been charged with two counts of aggravated assault with a deadly weapon (the weapon being my vehicle).

I began to consider my options. I was now looking at seven or more years in prison. Fortunately, I had support from my family and administrative help from my employer and the Nursing Board. But I remained in denial about my alcoholism.

Through a difficult process of negotiation, my attorney helped me work out a plea agreement with the state. I agreed to make a guilty plea with three and a half years of incarceration and three years of probation. I began to mentally prepare and get my affairs in order prior to my sentencing date. I surrendered my nurse's license voluntarily and was placed into custody in July of 2013. I had now lost everything, including the career I loved, all of my savings—and now, my freedom. Despite all that loss, I was still in denial.

The denial continued even after I got to prison. As they say in the program, I white-knuckled it. And I still believed that I did not have a problem; I was a normal person, like all the other people I knew who drank. The only difference was that I got caught. I continued this insane thinking as I did my time in prison. Often, I'd hear about AA meetings on my unit, but I was still telling myself that I was not one of "those" people.

That all changed when, a little over two years into my sentence, I had an emotional breakdown. I needed something that would numb me, to make these feelings go away. This was the first time in prison that I thought about actually drinking. I started crying and went to the phone to call my brother, who also is in recovery. He listened and let me talk until I calmed down, which was exactly what I needed. He asked if there were any AA meetings in the prison I could attend. He knew exactly what to say to me and knew what I needed to hear.

After I hung up, I reached out to a fellow inmate who I knew attended the AA meeting on my unit. She was thrilled that I was asking her about it and invited me to attend the next meeting with her. I went to my first AA meeting in October of 2015 in prison.

The AA volunteer who brought in the meeting that day was new to our prison. She introduced herself, welcomed newcomers and began with the readings. She asked the group if she could share her story with us since it was her first time meeting us. I listened as she spoke. I could relate to everything she said and felt. This was the first time in years that I did not feel alone. I realized at that moment that maybe I was an alcoholic. A flood of emotions came over me. I left that meeting with a Big Book, a "Twelve and Twelve" and other literature. I knew I had found something.

I continued to go to that AA meeting every week. I looked forward to it. The lady who told her story shared the meeting duties with two other women. About a month from my release, I was hoping to see her again. However, she did not come back before I left. I knew the rules and knew she was not allowed to provide her contact information to me upon my release, but I also knew I needed to thank her for what she had done for me. I was worried I'd never be able to tell her how much her story meant to me and how it impacted my life and my journey in AA.

In July of 2016, I was released from prison and started to attend AA meetings around my home until I found one I liked enough to make it my home group. At the time, this group happened to be doing service at a huge Grapevine convention. I wanted to help out because Grapevine meant a lot to me while I was locked up. One of my fellow inmates would always share her copies with me and I loved the stories.

At the conference, I volunteered in the hospitality room. After the first day doing service there, I headed out for the day. As I was leaving the hotel, I saw a woman standing at a booth. I did a double-take and realized that it was her, the volunteer who had shared her story that day in the prison, my very first meeting.

As I walked up to her, she recognized me immediately. I started to cry and told her that I had been afraid I was never going to be able to thank her for what she did. I told her how her story had impacted me and how it made me feel like I was not alone anymore. I told her that if I had never gone to prison, it's possible I wouldn't be alive now and it's possible I would still be living my life in misery.

I'm so grateful for finding AA in that prison and for the volunteers who brought those meetings in to us. They helped save my life, and taught me to trust my Higher Power, get honest and grow up.

Oh, and one more thing. I eventually was able to get reinstated, and I'm now working again as a nurse. Thank you, AA.

A.W.
Glendale, Arizona

Unlocking Stories

August 2016

A friend of mine has been taking a meeting into a women's prison for some time now. It's quite a commitment in time and effort. The drive to the prison alone from her home is more than one hour because of bumper-to-bumper, rush-hour traffic. Then she must go through the usual security clearance at the prison. There have even been times that she has made the long drive only to be told that the prison is in lock-down or that her paperwork cannot be found.

She set up the format of the prison meeting to be a Grapevine meeting, just like one she attends at her home group. She reads a story from the magazine and then the women share their own stories of experience, strength and hope. The women's stories have helped my friend to stay sober. Always there are extra copies of Grapevine for the women to read later. There's other literature too, but the Grapevines are the first to go, as they're colorful and easy to carry and read.

She was so moved by the women's stories that she asked them if they would be interested in sharing them with Grapevine. The women were excited but they were not sure how to go about writing their stories. That's where my story begins. My friend asked me to help. Me? Go into the prison?

Since I am not a writer or a teacher, I wondered how I could be of service. But I've learned in AA that willingness and an open mind are very important. So I asked around and reached out to others more qualified in writing and teaching to get advice. Then I went through the usual clearance, called the person at the prison who would approve the workshop and, before I knew it, the day had come to "carry the message."

To be honest, I was not the least bit afraid of the prisoners. It was the prison guards that had me feeling intimidated. Did they have my clearance? Would they let me through?

Once we were inside the compound, we were bussed to the unit where the meeting would be held. I have attended meetings at treatment centers, juvenile facilities, homeless shelters and hospitals. By far the women at this meeting were more excited to hear the message of AA than any others I'd seen. They understood the importance of giving back, sharing their experience, their strength and their hope. They wanted to share their stories to help other alcoholics.

I brought with me information from the www.aagrapevine.org website about the guidelines for publishing stories in Grapevine. I gave the women a few suggestions on how to get started. I told them that, although they might not think they were great writers, everyone had a powerful story. All they needed to do was try and the words would come. I shared my experience of having my work published and of the nicest rejection letters I have ever received.

After the meeting, I left with a full heart. I felt hope for the women I had just met. Hope for their future and hope that they too will be able to carry the message to other alcoholics. I believe that one day, at least one of them will see her story published in Grapevine.

Anonymous

No Mint on My Pillow
June 2014

I was two years sober when I landed back inside a jail after not getting into trouble for eight years. I hadn't done time for what I had done before, but I thought that if I stayed out of trouble, my crime would eventually go away. That was wishful thinking.

One day in June 2012 I woke up early to loud banging on my apartment door. I asked my fiancé to see who it was. It was the cops. After being arrested and sitting in a holding cell for more than 24 hours, I was introduced to my new home. Getting put in jail is a scary experience. But being in jail as a sober person can be a life-changing experience.

I had forgotten how crazy it can get inside a women's prison: there's always chaos and noise day and night. The food actually had gotten worse since my last visit to this esteemed facility, and there was certainly no little mint on the pillow from housekeeping to welcome me to my cell. Instead, there were rules to follow and a bedtime. There were no good movies to watch, nor was there the mighty cell phone to occupy the time.

AA meetings were mostly used to get off the block to socialize, but a few women took them seriously. When I heard the announcement, I couldn't get up the stairs fast enough. I found myself sharing my experience, strength and hope with several women, and I got the chance to hear more about them.

Several weeks after arriving at this prison, I was sent to the state that wanted me. Pulling up to the gate of the prison and seeing those ominous steel doors creep open was an eye-opener. This was really happening. I wasn't dreaming.

I discovered that being in a cell for 20 hours a day can feel like hell to some, but my Higher Power sat beside me every step of the way. Prayer and meditation didn't sound so foreign to me. Now they became a daily routine. Many times my cellmate would find me on my bunk in tears. I was OK, though: I knew that I would get through it and eventually go home.

Asking about AA literature and meetings was difficult to say the least—there were none. Several women in the block were drawn to me and asked me how I didn't lose my mind. When I mentioned that my Higher Power stayed with me day and night, they lit up and realized I was in some kind of a program. We spoke of recovery and AA, and since there were no meetings at this facility we formed our own group. I offered my knowledge and sense of hope to these women. My Higher Power helped me realize that was why I was put in prison and what I was meant to do.

A month later, I got to go home. I was sad to leave my girls, but I also couldn't wait to have my freedom back. The first thing I did when I got home—besides having a wonderful meal—was to go to an AA meeting where I was asked to speak. Service—what a great experience!

I'm still in touch with a few of the women I met, whether they are in or out of prison. I'm so grateful for what AA has taught me, and for the opportunity to help other alcoholics. If you decide to go into a prison to carry the message, remember that you may be the only Big Book someone ever sees.

Michelle G.
Philadelphia, Pennsylvania

Keeping It Real

July 2018

In 2002, I had my first stay in the Butler County Prison in Pennsylvania. I was 23. I never thought in a million years that I would be incarcerated. I thought I was too young to go to jail because of my drinking.

I was lying there, sick on the floor, in a portable bed they called a "boat," because the jail was so overcrowded. I was thinking about what a bunch of losers all of these other women around me were. Why didn't they quit doing such stupid things to keep coming back? I just couldn't identify. I underestimated the power of alcohol.

As I sat in there for a few weeks, I decided that I was never coming back. I was going to quit drinking and change my life. So I started attending the meetings in the jail that were brought in by members of AA. Two women in particular, Renee and Becky, carried the message in to us on a regular basis.

Over time, I began to identify with them. They kept it real. I needed that. I needed to see that we were very much alike in our experiences when we drank. I can still remember, as I close my eyes now, how I felt at those meetings in the jail library, with Renee and Becky sharing their experiences with us. The language of the heart traveled from their hearts and landed in mine.

And yet after I was released, I still had to return to that jail multiple times.

Finally, in 2003, I landed back in there when I was five months pregnant. I looked around and remembered how I felt that first time, thinking what losers all of those women were. Then all of a sudden, the thought struck me: Jamie, you're a loser too. But somehow I knew I was not a loser, I was an alcoholic. And they were alcoholics, just like me.

I remembered about the phenomenon of craving and the obsession of the mind. I understood why all of us kept coming back. It wasn't stupid things we were doing. Well, maybe the actions that got us into jail were stupid, but the real problem was that we couldn't put the drink down once we picked it up. I knew in that moment that alcohol was going to kill me.

During my time between jail visits, I had attended AA meetings. I knew AA had something I wanted, but I was just coming to meetings to socialize and pick up a boyfriend. But this time, as I sat there in the jail meeting, I began to hear what other members said. For the first time, the seed of sobriety secretly slipped into my spirit and began to grow. It was like a beautiful song that finally made sense to me.

That was my last trip to the Butler County Prison as an inmate. During my first year sober, I couldn't wait to get off probation and go back and take AA meetings into that jail. Two years later it finally happened, and I haven't stopped since.

I can still remember Becky and Renee and the stories they shared with us. I use their actions as a model today, as my guide to carry the message to these women. Now I'm keeping it real. Keeping it "as real as real gets" helps me to focus on my own sense of gratitude for AA.

I'm totally convinced that this Butler County women's jail meeting is the best meeting around. There's no way to fully convey what God sends me home with when I leave there. I experience a big ball of gratitude, identification and empathy. And yes, sometimes frustration, as I watch some of the women return again and again, just as I did.

Most importantly, I know in my heart that I will certainly return there as an inmate if I stop carrying the message and forget where I came from. I feel that God has definitely revealed his real purpose for me. I will be forever grateful for the criminal justice system and that jail. It actually saved my life. It gave me a moment to take a hard, long look at myself and see how messed up my life was. That's when Alcoholics Anonymous crept in and showed me that I don't have to live like that anymore and that there is a solution to have a beautiful life.

Jamie M.
Butler, Pennsylvania

A Letter From Prison

July 2017

Prison has been a rewarding experience for me. Time in here has helped me build a strong, sturdy foundation in recovery. I do not regret anything. I have forgiven myself for all my past transgressions. Everything happened this way for a reason. Now that I know God has a plan for me, it's easier to stay on track.

Prior to prison, I had a tiny taste of "the good life." With only 11 months of sobriety, I believed I could take on the world. I was motivated, worked a full time job, took care of my daughter, went to a ton of AA meetings, did service, worked at conventions and created real friendships within the Fellowship.

Then, somewhere along the line, I got too confident. I moved out of my sober living house, cut back on meetings, didn't do what my sponsor suggested and began dating random guys. I believed I could do it all on my own. I was wrong.

I relapsed within a week of moving out. Soon I quit my job and ignored all my family and friends. It was horrible. Remorse and guilt overwhelmed me. I had abandoned happiness for despair. My addiction flew out of control and I landed here in this Arizona Prison serving a six and a half-year sentence.

Yet today I have never been happier. It may sound unbelievable, but it's true. I have a personal freedom today I never believed I could obtain. AA has given me a second chance at life. I've spent my time in here learning about who I really am. Recovery has completely changed me for the better. I've never been so stable and grounded.

The men and women of AA who take the time out of their lives to bring us meetings are an inspiration. They give me hope for the future. Some have been to prison or jail before and now come back to help others. I plan to do an H & I commitment when I'm released in 2019. I look forward to sharing my experience, strength and hope with others.

Currently, we have six meetings in my yard. Only two of them have outside people who chair; the other four are chaired by two wonderful women named Colby and Mel. They are inmates just like me. These women have touched many of our lives. One of our meetings has up to 170-plus women.

Recovery is hard work, but the rewards of sobriety make every day worth living. I have an amazing sponsor who tells me how it is. Today I can be honest with myself and others. I've done my Steps twice in the last two years, and each time I remember more. My family has forgiven me and my 7-year-old daughter and I are best friends again.

I love the woman I have become. I look in the mirror and love who looks back at me now. I pray all the time. Meditating has proven to be a challenge for me, but I refuse to give up. Working with others and doing the next right thing gives me joy. Thank God there is a solution.

Anonymous

A Clear Signal
July 2013

In early 2009, I had almost a year of sobriety. I had rebuilt relationships with my family, gained trust, found fellowship with a group of AAs and earned the material comforts that I had lost over the course of years of alcohol abuse.

I felt "normal," like I didn't need the program anymore. I made every excuse to skip meetings until I gradually stopped attending altogether. Instead, I found myself back in my old neighborhood, in an old friend's house, getting wasted next to the clear TV that he had recently brought home from prison. It was the kind of clear appliance in which an inmate can't hide contraband, and it wasn't the first time I had seen one set up in a friend's house like a novelty item. With a head full of AA, I stared at his TV and sank into my relapse.

How did we end up here? How does a group of suburban kids decide to waste their potential and either die from substance abuse or settle into a pattern of buying clear TVs on each trip back to the penitentiary?

Within a few months I lost everything all over again: the job, the car, the feeling of waking up without withdrawal symptoms or a hangover. Sober friends offered to get me into treatment—I politely told them I wasn't finished drinking.

On July 9, 2009, I was driving down a two-lane suburban back road after a typical day of consuming just enough liquor and pills to still be able to function. I fell asleep behind the wheel, crossed the centerline and hit a motorcycle coming from the opposite direction. I killed an innocent man who was driving home to his wife and 15-year-old daughter.

I spent the following year in a county jail trying to wrap my mind around the idea that I had taken a person's life, that a young girl would grow up without her father. I tried to focus on exercise, meditation and teaching myself Spanish, but then I felt guilty for moving on too easily. I felt guilty just for being alive.

I found refuge in a weekly AA meeting at the jail, and there I met an amazing sponsor. She helped me feel comfortable sharing all the emotions that I experienced after seeing my victim's family in court, and she taught me how to do the best I could to try to make amends for an offense that I felt didn't seem forgivable.

After my conviction, I was transferred to a medium security women's prison in central Illinois. My sponsor gave me a Big Book, a "Twelve and Twelve," and a book of daily reflections. My aunt also sent me a Grapevine subscription. I moved into a loud, chaotic environment where housing units held 100 women in five dorms.

I kept to myself initially, but after a few months, I noticed two women sitting at the end table in the day room with a Big Book between them. I asked to join them and since that day, we've met every Sunday at an AA meeting. Once a month I bring the most recent Grapevine and we share our thoughts on the discussion topic. Some weeks we can gather as many as seven people; on others there are fewer, but the three of us are always there.

I still struggle with self-forgiveness, but I know that the Promises are happening in my life. I am in better shape physically, mentally and spiritually than ever before. I've also learned the importance of rigorous honesty. I have amazing relationships with my family and my boyfriend. I correspond with my sponsor through the mail, and I have been blessed to pass her wisdom along to my new sponsee.

I am writing this story in a composition notebook on a metal stand that also holds my clear TV and my Grapevines. I have two years remaining on my sentence. When I am released I plan to leave behind the TV—and take my Grapevine subscription with me.

Anonymous

Watching It Grow
July 2017

I have been taking meetings into prison for about 13 years now. It keeps me close to the middle of AA, where we are truly needed.

Six years ago, I was given the opportunity to help take a weekly meeting into the minimum general population at a women's prison. It was an open discussion meeting led by the women. We brought in Big Books and Grapevines, and when things got off track, one of us would share and try to bring things back to AA. Occasionally we had a gal who would get serious about working the Steps and we might get through the first five with her in anticipation of her release date.

Then a few years ago, the meeting started to change. One gal in particular started talking about her experience with the Steps. And then she started sponsoring other women. Apparently she had been sponsored by a woman who was recently released who was sponsored by a woman on the outside. An amazing chain of sponsorship began to grow.

One evening, one of the women spoke about waking up and hearing voices talking quietly in her dorm. She sat up and looked around to see where they were coming from and discovered a couple of women from the meeting huddled up at a table with their books open, talking about the Steps. I got goose bumps. That's when I realized that our role as volunteers had changed. What they most needed from us was the tools of AA so that they could work the program and have access to the bigger AA community.

The women even held business meetings and registered the group with the General Service Office. They anxiously waited until the package came. It was so emotional reading the letter from New York at the meeting. I was so proud of what these women were doing. We volunteers had been bringing a meeting in to them for an hour every week; now they brought Alcoholics Anonymous into the facility 24 hours a day, seven days a week! And only inside members of AA can do that.

A couple of years have passed now. Several women in that sponsorship chain are now living on the outside and are sober. I know where each one is today. That's the miracle of our program. It's been amazing to watch what these women have accomplished with each other through AA. Who would want to miss an experience like this?

Annalee P.
Portland, Oregon

4

Walking the Walk

Using AA's Twelve Steps to grow in sobriety

G etting and staying sober takes work—work the AA members in this chapter were willing to do. Using the guidance laid out in AA's Twelve Steps, the pathway to sobriety got clearer and clearer for these prisoners, even through the pain that often comes with growth. Says Jesse C. in the story "More at Peace," "I did my First Step sitting on my prison bunk one day, realizing I wanted to die because I couldn't see any other way the pain would end."

Desperation often drives us to reach out for help, and the AA program is there when we do. As Todd P. says in "Working on the Inside," "AA in prison is based on the same principles as AA on the outside"—it's just necessary to pick up the tools of sobriety and use them. The Steps and the sponsors many of the AAs in this chapter were able to connect with provide a blueprint to recovery. "I found out that I could learn how to live through the suffering of imprisonment. I found out that spiritual advancement was possible, even in here," says Todd.

But it takes work—and willingness. "When I got to prison this time, I was a beaten man and was willing to try anything," says C.T. in "While I Was in Prison." "My sponsor, Jim M., told me I could stay sober through the Twelve Steps, but I had to be willing to go to any lengths." For one of the members in this chapter, that meant taking a Fifth Step with a cellmate who spoke a different language.

Taking a "searching and fearless" inventory can dig up some difficult truths about a person, but it can also be the turning point in an alcoholic's life—a moment when the future spins from fear to hope.

"This inventory-taking was the turning point of my life," writes R.R. in the story "Freedom Began in Prison." "It was during this time that I learned what true freedom was. It had nothing to do with walls and guards—it had to do with a feeling inside."

More at Peace

June 2020

I was raised by parents who got sober when I was young. By age 13, I had experimented with liquor and gotten into trouble at school, which led my father to take me along with him to AA meetings. He didn't trust me at home. I kept coming to the meetings because of a beautiful girl my age who also attended. I didn't work the Steps; nor did I recognize the depth of my disease nor understand just how low it would take me.

By 16, I wanted to relate to my peers. I wanted to drink and feel young. I stopped going to meetings and was kicked out of my father's house. I did well in school and appeared OK on the outside. My drinking worsened. There was an ER visit, a few 911 calls and a lot of people hurt in my wake.

A few weeks after my 18th birthday, I committed a robbery and, separately, shot two people in a dispute. I was sentenced to 32 years. I needed to address my disease, but I justified putting that off because I had so much time to serve.

I spent 13 years bouncing between wet and dry before I ended up at a spiritual bottom and finally accepted my need for AA. I did my First Step sitting on my prison bunk one day, realizing I wanted to die because I couldn't see any other way the pain would end. I reached out and found a sponsor, someone I had known in school who was actually one of the first people I got roaring drunk with as a boy.

I was fortunate to be at a prison that had weekly AA meetings. My Second and Third Steps involved me crying and cussing out the whole AA meeting as the guys argued about coffee and prison regulations. I struggled to find a power greater than myself that could restore me to sanity. The next week I felt a little better, a little more

OK with the chaos, a little more under the care and guidance of a Higher Power.

The Promises came true as I worked the Steps. Sitting in prison now, with more than a decade left to serve, I feel more at peace, more content and more connected than ever before. I've been given the opportunity to do Twelfth Step work in here, as I volunteer with mental health treatment. I also get to teach relapse prevention classes. I've also completed my bachelor's degree and graduated from my state Electrical Apprenticeship Program.

But mostly, today I'm a grateful recovering alcoholic. I am no longer afraid, nor am I alone.

Jesse C.
Dillwyn, Virginia

Working on the Inside

June 2020

'll never forget sitting on my bunk wondering what had happened. How did I get locked up in this cell?

Fourteen months earlier, I had walked into an AA meeting after I made a phone call to the AA hotline. I was drinking on a daily basis for over three years. I had been charged with a felony in a white-collar crime involving hundreds of thousands of dollars. My drinking was no longer shielding me from the consequences of my behavior.

While I was at that first AA meeting, I read for the first time the Twelve Steps shade on the wall. It was the first time I understood that there was a spiritual component to my alcoholism. I count that moment as the start of my recovery. It was August 6, 2003.

My sentence hearing was 79 days later. In that small amount of time, I attended more than 150 AA meetings and managed to stay sober. I was sentenced to 14 years with a possibility of parole after four.

My first year in prison was full of shame and anxiety caused by tension between my obligations. On one hand, I was in a new environment, rebuilding my life in prison. On the other, I was very much aware that I had left my four children and their mother with no means of support. I was full of shame over what my family was going through, and I was haunted by how my time in prison would affect them.

AA in prison is based on the same principles as AA on the outside. The difference is, in here we don't usually have any oldtimers to pass down the understanding of the Steps and Traditions. At that time, there were no outside AA service members assigned to our prison. We were left with what we could decipher out of the Big Book and our *Twelve Steps and Twelve Traditions* book on our own. This always turned into colorful discussions because we were all new to recovery and struggled with understanding the Steps and Traditions.

Today in my home group, when I share my story I will ask, "Have you ever seen a fistfight in an AA meeting? Well, I have." The meetings we ran in prison were a gift burdened by our inexperience with the program of AA. Our meetings taught all of us to personalize our recovery as best we could to our own understanding, using the Steps and Traditions to guide us.

Sitting on my bunk a year into my sentence, I took stock. I had managed to stay sober, work a prison job and regain my health. I found my way back to the faith of my youth in here. Thanks to the literature, I continued to work the Steps with my fellow inmates on a weekly basis. It was in these weekly meetings that I learned the value of doing a fearless and thorough moral inventory of my past, as described in the Fourth Step. The first time I and the other guys completed a Fourth or Fifth Step with each other, our work was not very fearless or thorough, yet it was enough to keep us sober. We revisited these two Steps multiple times while incarcerated.

Identifying character defects in the Sixth Step turned out to be one of the most empowering awareness Steps for me. We printed out definitions of the "seven deadly sins" and worked at matching our behaviors to these definitions. Asking God to remove those defects of character took a lot of meditation and prayer.

The Tenth, Eleventh and Twelfth Steps are the enduring points in my recovery. I found out that I could learn how to live through the suffering of imprisonment. I found out that spiritual advancement was possible, even in here. I found out that I could not only endure, but I could endure well. I saw that my suffering had value. I challenged myself to focus my efforts where I could make a difference, not only in my life, but in the lives of others, especially my children's.

I stayed connected with my children through visits, phone calls and letters. I can be honest with them about my alcoholism. I tell the truth and back it up with my behavior, providing us with a good foundation that continues today. I continue to focus on the values and strength I acquired in prison, along with my growing health and spirituality.

Finally, I was granted a year's reduction in my sentence and my parole hearing date was set. I was so grateful to be released from prison after 1,095 days of incarceration. It was now time for me to implement my recovery and these skills in the outside world.

My first year out on parole was full of mixed emotions. I was happy to be out of prison, but fearful of what the future held. I was able to keep up with my recovery and my AA meetings while I found work as a carpenter. Over time, I came to terms with my faith as I rebuilt trust with my children. I allowed the positive aspects of my parents and family to influence my life. I let family and friends see my failures and talk about them, rather than trying to hide them. I established relationships and I was able to keep them. I was able to remarry and develop that relationship as well. All these Promises came to me.

After serving my three years in prison, at the age of 46 I enrolled as a freshman at our local university. I was determined to use what I had learned about myself and my alcoholism to help others who have faced the same challenges and struggles. I received a bachelor's degree in social work in 2011 and went on to graduate school. In 2012, I received a master's degree in social work. I was 51 and starting over with a new career and a new life.

I was hired as a therapist by a national behavioral health company that focuses on mental health and addiction. Within a year, I was promoted as program director, and two years after that I was promoted as chief operating officer. Today I can help those who suffer with mental and physical health issues that come with addictions.

In 2016, I was released from my 10-year parole sentence. I am now free in every sense of the word and have become a better version of myself by staying close to AA and integrating the Twelve Steps into my life. Thanks to AA, I was able to hold on long enough to let the miracle happen to me and my family.

Todd P.
Bountiful, Utah

Inside Job
July 2017

I was introduced to AA in 2001 right at the start of my prison term. I got a sponsor through the Corrections Correspondence Service. He was a great guy, but he passed away only five months after we connected. Then I was blessed to be connected to his sponsor, who is still my sponsor today. He also takes AA meetings into New York State prisons.

This man has been there for me through my several journeys through the Steps, each time getting closer and closer to the root of why I could not stop drinking.

In 2009, when I was 42 and had five years sober, I had a nervous breakdown. I went on suicide watch with my arms cut up. I believed I could no longer live. I didn't know who I was. I had been through so many years of sexual abuse. It was truly the lowest point in my life.

While on suicide watch, I came to understand that I had never completely worked Step Three. It was then that I decided to finally turn my will and my life over to the care of God. I began to trust the mental health people at the prison. I was given a private therapist, who I believe helped save my life. I was able to process all the emotional pain and suffering and finally come to terms with who I am.

Today I'm a happy and sober transgender woman. But I also now deal with new obstacles, such as discrimination and masculinization from both inmates and staff. Many times I've come close to relapsing, but by using the tools of the program and "going to any lengths," I have survived those close calls. My sponsor suggested I write my story, as he has been a Grapevine contributor himself.

I also have a female sponsor in here now. She lives in my parole region. She's awesome. One alcoholic helping another

Alcoholics Anonymous and complete honesty and willingness, coupled with courage, has given me my life back. I am sober and happy.

I go to meetings regularly, and I share my experience, strength and hope with the other inmates no matter what other people say or feel about me.

Patty S.
Chino, California

Our Mutual Friend

Online Exclusive
July 2014

I'm not very good at robbing banks. My track record staying sober isn't so hot either. The former is the reason I'm writing this from a federal lock-up. The latter has me using this time to try and work my Steps...again. Step Four always seems to be where I get stuck.

The facility I'm in does not have any kind of organized AA meetings, so I'm on my own. At least that's what I thought until I found out it was possible for me to get a sponsor via the mail through the GSO Corrections Correspondence Service.

I got a very encouraging and down-to-earth sponsor. He walked me through the first three Steps in short order. This brought me back to my previous roadblock: a fearless and searching moral inventory. To me, there was nothing fearless about taking an inventory of myself.

It wasn't easy, but with my sponsor's guidance, I completed Step

Four. Because my sponsor read my inventory when I sent it to him, I chalked up Step Five, too. At the time, he was the only other human being I felt I could share it with. I felt good about overcoming what I considered a major hurdle and moved on.

My sponsor encouraged me to keep my written inventory in the hope that I'd find someone in prison to share it with. Given the lack of AA meetings here and that I try to keep to myself, I didn't see that happening.

That was until my new cellie moved in. He was a Polish citizen awaiting extradition to his country. The only English words he knew were the standard profanities. The only Polish I was familiar with was the Polish sausage my hometown of Chicago is famous for. Needless to say, our conversations were pretty much nonexistent. That is, until one day I was in the cell reading my Big Book and starting to fall asleep. My cellmate yelled out, "Beeg Book! Is good, Dan."

Through a series of creative pantomimes, I learned that my new Polish friend was himself in AA. Turns out he had been sober for about 10 years. What a small world!

Well, out came my moral inventory. What transpired was as cathartic as it was humorous. It took several hours, some sign language that was at times as vulgar as it was creative, and some patience, but I shared my Fourth Step inventory face-to-face with another human being. It may have been a bit unusual, but it felt great!

The whole experience really touched me. It showed me that all of us who are lucky enough to count ourselves as AA members share a universal language.

Dan G.
Chicago, Illinois

While I Was in Prison

April 2012

Like it says on page 33 of the Big Book, "One doesn't necessarily have to drink a long time nor take the quantities some of us have." I am 42 years old and have spent the last 11 years in and out of prison due to my alcoholism. When I was younger, I felt I didn't fit in. Then I started drinking and all my fears vanished. I thought I could have everything—women, money, my dreams—the sky was the limit.

But at some point in my youth, alcohol turned on me and I crossed that invisible line from having fun to not having anybody who wanted to be around me. I had three DUIs by the 12th grade and still, I couldn't see the unmanageability. On the last DUI, the judge made me go to AA meetings and I could see why you guys were there and I wasn't: You needed it and I didn't.

In a geographic, I moved from North Carolina to South Carolina and there I found I could control my drinking if I drank during business hours only. That didn't last and blackouts became a way of life for me. I was left with the bewilderment of blackouts: what happened, who I might've hurt, how I got home and where I left my truck.

I eventually became unemployed and unemployable. I found after drinking that I could do a break-in and get money to keep drinking. I did just over four years in prison the first time I was caught. When I got out, I got back on my plan—which got me drunk. Anything I do on my own is trouble. I stayed out of jail for eight months, but now I'm back with a seven year sentence. It's all due to my drinking and self-will run riot. It took 25 years of drinking to see how I was a tornado winding through the lives of my parents, wife and children.

It took prison, AA and a program called Bridging the Gap for me to finally find myself. When I got to prison this time, I was a beaten man and was willing to try anything. I wrote to AA and they sent me a Big Book and hooked me up with a sponsor. I wasn't alone in my alcoholism. My sponsor, Jim M., told me I could stay sober through the Twelve Steps, but I had to be willing to go to any lengths.

I totally understand why the Steps are in the order they are. I found that admission was the key to seeing the powerlessness and unmanageability of my life. Then Jim showed me Step Two and that "deep down in every man, woman and child is the fundamental idea of God." In Step Three, I learned that I couldn't be the lead actor because I couldn't get the players to do as I wanted. I had to quit playing God and let God be the director and agent of my life. Jim told me that although we were so far apart—he was in New York City and I was in North Carolina—we could still take this Step together just by picking a date and time. I was in awe at how willingness, open-mindedness and honesty are the keys.

After Step Three, we launched onto a course of rigorous action. There was a lot of pain in the Fourth Step and a lot of stuff I never told anyone in my life, but I know that stuff will get you drunk. There were times when I thought my fears of self-appraisal would do me in, but I agreed at the beginning that I would go to any lengths for victory over alcohol. I honestly, without reservation, took Step Four and when the time came to do Step Five, Jim set up a whole day to come from New York City to the prison.

On that day, he brought a cheeseburger, fries and two pieces of pie. We are allowed food if it's an outside visit. I felt when I laid eyes on him that I'd known him forever. I poured out my life through words and crying. My Higher Power was holding me by the hand that day and showing me that anything was possible in sobriety.

I asked Jim how I could ever repay him for what he did and I will never forget his words: "Just do the same for another alcoholic." I know it was hard for me to understand why someone would come all the way from New York to North Carolina to help someone like me. I'll never forget Jim M.'s words when I was bawling like a baby. He said, "You are a good guy, a good father and you have been sick for a long time."

After taking this Step and accepting the unconditional love of AA, I saw that a world of opportunity is available for me as long as I take the simple suggestions.

Bridging the Gap showed me that no matter the circumstances, I can start picking up the pieces of my life and establish long-lost relationships with loved ones. It's hard for me to put into words what a beautiful gift AA and that program has been to me. Today, I get to put on civilian clothes and go to AA meetings in the community where I'll be living.

At the meetings, I find people just like me, just different shapes, sizes, colors and names. These people care. AA cares. I feel I'm no longer a burden to society, no longer terrorizing the community, and I no longer have to take chances playing Russian Roulette while drinking and driving.

In prison, I know a new freedom and a new happiness. I do not regret the past nor wish to shut the door on it. My whole attitude and outlook on life has changed and God is doing for me what I could not do myself. I had a visit from my son and my daughter and that hasn't happened in a long time. I can only thank God and AA. Today, though I am incarcerated, life is beautiful.

C.T.
North Carolina

The Chop Shop
July 2013

I loved Big Bill. So did a lot of people. He was a motorcycle man. And he loved giving pretty girls a ride. Bill is no longer with us because he's now gone on to that Big Ride in the Sky, but not before helping many, many folks. He sponsored men, helped out in meetings and was always there for people. He had a solid program.

There was even a time when I needed a place to stay, and Bill offered that I could move in with him. He said he would take his bike out of the shed so I could park my own motorcycle there instead. I told him I'd made other plans, and for a while he nursed a resentment, but eventually he got over himself. After all, he was the one who came up with the crazy idea of an "Amenda-Gram" service, where there would be a sliding fee according to the severity of the amend you were going to make. Bill did have a sense of humor.

Some years prior to this, Bill and I were sitting in his living room when he mentioned that at about eight or nine years into his sobriety he had to go to prison for a year. This was his Ninth Step work, part of cleaning up the past, he informed me. At the time I was about two years sober and it was hard to wrap my brain around his time in jail. I asked him about the experience, how it was for him, and he told me each of us had actually done time in the "joint," long before we got sober. This was just not who we were anymore. It was a solemn moment. Then he told me how grateful he was for Alcoholics Anonymous, how he relied on the program and the help of his Higher Power. This resonated with truth, and I was amazed.

Little did I know that one day this would be me! On this past January 15, the very day of my nine-year AA birthday, I found myself sitting in the county lock-up waiting for the "chain" to take me to the penitentiary for a year. I was in court the day prior for a charge that had carried over from my active days. I knew I had to face the music and take care of the past regardless of the outcome, but this certainly was not what I'd wanted. Thank God for my sponsor, my family and for many friends in the program, whose love and support would surely help me through this ordeal.

So far I've made it through a month and a half in prison. I have gotten past the initial culture shock, but let's face it—being locked up is hell. I am now 100 miles away from home, waiting until I finish out my time. This place is crazy. I am surrounded by the ever-present prison mentality and dangerous personalities. Somebody is always going to "the hole."

But we have meetings in here. Our outside AA "sponsors" come in to hold meetings on Tuesday and Thursday evenings, and on Saturday mornings we have a Big Book Step study. We are even allowed to brew up a pot of coffee. We're fortunate indeed. Average attendance at our "New Boundaries" meeting is 20 to 30 men. Several of us are working in sponsorship and completing the Steps.

My "cellie," Humble Joe, and I run the Chop Shop, where fellas come by to "chop it up" for the meeting after the meeting. We have had some spiritual experiences. For years on the outside I was imprisoned by this malady of ours. But now, in prison, I can experience a wonderful sense of freedom because of our program. I thank my Higher Power and ask for guidance, humility and acceptance, and I am grateful.

It was getting time for me to do another Fourth Step and I wanted to do it while still here to see what that would look like. Since my sponsor at home doesn't travel up here, our DCM came during a visiting period and we went over it for a Fifth Step. It was truly a spiritual experience.

Being asked to sponsor a man is an honor. I'm currently working with a fellow and we're approaching Step Three. As I contemplate my release date I find that I'm concerned about having enough time to get through the Steps with him. We'll do what we can and then he can continue with one of the other men in our crew. We're all in this together and there exists a sense of unity.

What I don't know is what this all means, what the purpose of my being here is. Someday perhaps I will understand this experience in a different way. What I do know is that I will leave this place, and go out unafraid. I will gravitate to meetings because AA has become part of my life. Our meetings are a way-station, a safe haven, a place to gain strength. A good friend told me that God has a plan, even if I don't know what it is. Also I can tell you that I have not had the desire, the obsession, the compulsive preoccupation to drink or use, and for that I am truly grateful.

Soon I'll be rejoining my community, my family, my home group and my many friends in AA. How I love them and long for their fellowship and all the things we do together on the outside! They have visited me, written letters, brought coffee for our meetings. We talk on the phone and I have experienced a lot of AA events vicariously. Because of the amends I've been able to make, my son came to live at my place so I wouldn't have to worry about my things while I was gone.

A couple of the fellas went over to my garage the other day to start and run my motorcycle, to make sure we're good to go! I can hardly wait. And I am imagining Bill on his bike on the Big Ride...with a pretty angel on the back. See you on the road or at a meeting!

Michael W.
Monroe, Washington

Freedom Began in Prison
February 1970

The Starlight Bowl is a lovely outdoor concert auditorium, set deep between canyon walls, high above "beautiful downtown Burbank" in California. This summer night held particular significance for me. My ten-year-old daughter Cindy was with me, her silky golden hair spread over my knees as she rested her head on my lap. We were listening to the delightful strains of "Tales From the Vienna Woods" at a concert by the Burbank Symphony Orchestra.

It hadn't always been this way...

Several years before this memorable night, I was released from a state prison, a stranger to my daughter and very apprehensive about how I'd behave in free society. I'd never been able to cope with freedom before.

Six years before my release, I stood at the bar in a local tavern with a pistol in my hand. I was a practicing alcoholic and desperately needed money to continue my latest drunk. Being too proud to beg, having run out of friends and family, and feeling the fantastic courage granted by much red wine, I was attempting robbery. Fortunately for the bar owner (and, as it turned out, for me), I was captured in the midst of my bumbling crime. The police treated me fairly, even kindly. The court procedures passed swiftly, and within three months I was on the way to a state prison. I was to remain there three years.

This three-year period became the greatest, most productive time I'd spent in all my 30 years up to that point. During my confinement, I again became active in my church, relearning many basic precepts of good living. I used the library facilities intensely, reading widely on philosophy and alcoholism. Most important of all, I became an involved, active participant in AA.

Delving deeply into the Twelve Steps under the adept guidance of the free AA members who came in twice a week, I was soon writing my Fourth Step inventory. Having completed this written confession to myself, I made arrangements with the prison staff to have an outside AA member come in to hear my Fifth Step. We were provided with a private office and coffee, and spent three hours reviewing the sordid details of my past. It was the first such occurrence in that particular institution, and it worked out so well that many men since then have been able to complete their Fourth and Fifth Steps while still incarcerated.

This inventory-taking was the turning point of my life. An almost immediate freedom from all guilt and remorse came upon me. I was literally free from my past. It was during this time that I learned what true freedom was. It had nothing to do with walls and guards—it had to do with a feeling inside. Freedom is a state of mind.

Today, I cherish my physical and emotional freedom with all my heart and soul. In order of precedence, it stands second only to sobriety. What an education AA has given to me! Everything I am or have belongs to AA in reality. More than tangible benefits, AA has given me a way to go, a way to live and live happily and abundantly.

Many blessings have been showered upon me during my five years and nine months of sobriety—great spiritual gifts, as well as the more ordinary supplies of money and goods. These great gifts come one after the other in spite of my own foolishness and fumbling, as I very slowly grope my way toward the light of reason and love. The good things increase in direct proportion to my willingness to become more teachable and humble in my daily affairs.

And so it is that a chronic daily drunk, discarded by free society, hating and rejecting the very society that spawned him, can come to enjoy what many "free" people may take for granted: a simple concert, a wonderful summer night filled with beautiful music, and a sweet little child who loves and trusts her daddy.

R.R.
Universal City, California

Free on the Inside

June 2015

When I was 3, I had my first taste of liquor. By the age of 11, my alcoholic stepfather and I were getting drunk together. Although I was an alcoholic, I still lived a productive life. I have three children, a wife and my own tattoo business. My studio was always filled with alcoholics. I was getting drunk on the job and spiraling out of control, but I never knew why. The thought of getting help never occurred to me.

But on June 5, 2009, I had a spiritual awakening. I was shot twice by police officers and charged with aggravated assault of a public servant with a deadly weapon. I was drunk and high the day I was shot, and I came within seconds of dying. Looking back, I've come to believe a power greater than myself was looking over me. My Higher Power gave me a second chance.

A few weeks later, on July 29, I went to my very first AA meeting, by myself, in the county jail. It was there I met other alcoholics who were also seeking help. I learned to reach out, and I got a sponsor through AA World Services. With my new sponsor I made a searching and fearless moral inventory of myself so he and I could see my path of destruction, and I began to see my path to staying sober.

I've been corresponding with my AA sponsor Pat for four years now. He recently celebrated 27 years of sobriety. He took me through the Steps and has taught me many tools to stay sober. Through Step work, I learned things about myself I never knew, as well as my defects of character. I also learned to renew myself and gain a deeper understanding about myself. I've been granted the serenity to accept the things I cannot change, courage to change the things I can, and the wisdom to know the difference. Pat also introduced me to the best little magazine, called Grapevine. It's so encouraging to read it because it's filled with stories about people just like me.

I've been in here since June 5, 2009, and even though I have a life sentence, I am finally free on the inside. I now reach out to other alcoholics and share my experience to help others overcome this terrible disease of alcoholism, which I was once blind to. That is my message.

I've been sober for more than five years. That's the longest I've ever had since I was 9. My wife has also started going to AA meetings. Together we walk one day at a time through prayer and meditation. For both of us, our primary purpose is to stay sober and help other alcoholics achieve sobriety.

C.A.
Rosharon, Texas

A New Freedom
July 2019

I came into the program in 1997. At first I used women as my Higher Power, but in July of 1999, after two trips to prison and a lot more pain, something finally stuck and I got sober.

Good things started happening in my life. I got out and got married to a special woman who taught me what love really was. I soon became an assistant manager at a large retail store. I was going to AA meetings and I was involved in service at the local and area levels.

I was happy, but being the alcoholic that I am, I thought I only needed some of the Steps. I really didn't want to do all of them. I definitely didn't want to do the Fourth Step because that would mean a complete housecleaning, bringing up all the skeletons of my past. So it was not surprising that I started making decisions based on self. During that time, it was only by the grace of God that I didn't drink.

After one of those self-centered decisions, and with seven years of sobriety, I ended up in prison with a 17-year sentence hanging over my head. Fortunately, I was able to at least hold on to the honesty in my program, and when I went to court, I pleaded guilty without any plea deal because I didn't want to put my family through the pain of a trial. It was one of the few unselfish things I did during that time.

My Higher Power, being all-powerful, was still looking out for me. I only had to spend a very short amount of time in one of the most dangerous penitentiaries in the country. I was then transferred to another much less dangerous prison. Inmates at that place had fights and there were occasional stabbings, but it was nothing like the first prison.

When I first got to the new prison I thought, Man, I should start an AA meeting. I thought I knew so much about AA after my years of sobriety. I would take my Big Book up to a little room attached to the common area in the housing unit and sit for an hour, one day a week. I can't really remember what day of the week it was, but I did that for a month or two. I couldn't figure out why no one was coming up there to have me educate them about AA. Maybe it was because my own house wasn't in order; I really had nothing to offer someone else.

After I was there a year, the administrators started having an AA meeting brought in from the outside and I would go and share my "knowledge" with them. During this time I was so grateful that my Higher Power was with me, because on Mother's Day 2008, my mother passed away. It was only because I could feel my Higher Power there with me that I did not start drinking. Those people who think there isn't alcohol in prison have never been in prison. Alcohol was all around me—everywhere.

After about three years, I was transferred to another prison, one with a lower security level. When I got there, I heard they had an AA meeting. So of course I had to go and share my insight. I did that when it was convenient for me because the meeting was in the morning and sometimes I needed more sleep.

But one day I made it to the meeting and I heard someone sharing from the heart. He had that "light" that you see and hear in someone who's really working a program. The more I listened and watched, the more I knew that this guy was the real deal. I really wanted what he had.

After a couple of meetings, he asked me if he could take me through the Big Book. "We'll go through the book word-for-word," he said. "And I won't put any spin on it." At that time, I was in so much emotional pain and needed someone who I could trust to get some secrets off my chest. So I agreed.

We met one day a week to work through the Big Book. We even took the Steps in order, and when it came to taking the Fourth Step, it happened easily because I had done the first three Steps to the best of my ability. I can't say that it wasn't painful. It was. My sponsor told me that if I didn't do the Step both thoroughly and honestly, I was only hurting myself. He also said that if I did it right, it would be worth it. So I poured it all out on paper.

We met every day for a week or so. Soon, everything I had done and everybody I could remember was down on paper. A few days later, we met out on the bleachers on the yard and I did my Fifth Step. I read everything I had written down (I'm getting goose bumps writing this). My sponsor did not get up and run away screaming, "This guy is crazy!" He just sat there, listened and asked a few questions, and then we were done. Afterward, I felt a new freedom that words cannot describe. My Big Book now has two dates: July 3, 1999—the first day of my sobriety, and October 13, 2003—my first day of true freedom.

I'm still in prison and I don't do this thing perfectly. Still, I do my best each day to keep my side of the street clean. I use the tools that I have been given, now more than ever. Each day I try to help people and not hurt them. If I do something wrong, I try to fix it right then.

I've been given some very important gifts: 1) I have family who still love me and treat me well; 2) I get to live life on life's terms; and 3) I get the honor of taking other guys in prison through the Big Book and the Steps, exactly the way my sponsor did with me—with no spin on it.

Even though not all the guys I work with will stay sober, they still help me stay sober. I've had one guy make it clear through and he's now in the process of taking someone else through the book, while I've started again with someone else.

I never thought I would be able to say this, but here I am, in prison, behind a double-walled fence lined with concertina wire, and yet I'm freer now than I've ever been.

Here's an interesting miracle: When my sponsor had been convicted but not yet sentenced, the prosecutor said he wanted him to serve at least 10 years. In the end, the judge sentenced him to five. The whole time my sponsor was going through the court system, he kept going to AA meetings, helping other alcoholics and doing the things that his sponsor suggested. The day he was sentenced, the judge gave him a few days to get his affairs in order. On one of those days, he was talking to someone in his sponsorship chain and the man told him, "You are not being sentenced to prison, you're being called."

And that's where I met my sponsor, in prison. The miracle is that he was released after having been incarcerated far, far less than the five years he was sentenced to. I believe with all my heart that my loving Higher Power sent my sponsor to me because I was finally ready.

Jack R.
Marianna, Florida

100 Days to Go
July 2017

I've been in prison for four years, four months and 17 days, with exactly 100 days to go. I showed up here just barely sober after only 47 days in county. I was fresh off the streets with a violent, explosive attitude. I hated the world and everyone in it, including myself. I resented my father, mother and anyone else I could blame to justify my horrific alcoholic behavior. I was a victim and no one could convince me otherwise. I couldn't trust anyone either.

Since I had nothing to lose, I signed up for AA meetings on the medium security side, which allowed me to attend two meetings a month. It was just what I needed after coming out of a 10-year drunken binge. Two volunteers faithfully came every other Monday to bring us meetings. They became my rock in this lonely place. They even brought me a Big Book and a "Twelve and Twelve." I can't say I dove right in, but I did contemplate the new way of living these two AA people kept talking about.

My desire to want to learn more about AA got stronger and I began to ask if there were more meetings. I found one on every other Thursday, so now I was really doing it. Four meetings a month! I was big timing it.

I did this for nearly two and a half years. I was known by other inmates as "the woman in AA." I liked this label. If anyone had questions about recovery, they were sent to me. The naughty girls would even warn me not to go into certain parts of the prison when they were making pruno. They had respect for me and I began to respect myself. I still had no idea what I was doing really, but I just kept going back to meetings. These AAs had what I wanted. I became willing.

One day, I got moved over to minimum security. I had been hearing a lot of hype about a Monday night meeting there. When I walked through the doors, I zeroed in on two women who used to be over on the medium side with me. They used to mock me and roll their eyes because I "needed" AA. It turns out they were the big AA gurus over here! I figured there must be some kind of AA magic working if these two were welcoming me. So I dove in.

In just a couple of weeks, I learned more about working the Steps than I had in years. We met after the meetings to do Step work and discuss the business for our group, "Free on the Inside." We kept minutes, filled service positions and learned that our vote mattered. We have women in our group who have worked the Steps with outside sponsors through the visiting room and are now actively sponsoring women inside the walls. There was definitely a movement in recovery going on here, and I wanted in.

I asked one of the women I worked with in the welding shop to be my sponsor. I'd seen her for a while and believe me when I say I saw a huge difference in her when she began working the Steps. She was perfect for me. We spent the next year meeting on the yard, in the side yard of our unit, behind the welding shop, wherever we could get a minute. Through lots of tears, laughs, disagreements, breakthroughs and surrenders, I completed the Twelve Steps.

I've never experienced acceptance like this before. I've found my place in the world and it's in these rooms of AA. I have seen the beauty of this spiritual program. I hope one day to bring the message back inside these walls.

Michelle L.
Portland, Oregon

5

Sponsorship in Prison

When it comes to recovery, we don't have to do it alone—that's the message many of the members in this chapter relate. Sometimes it's a sponsor who carries AA's message of hope, sometimes a stranger. In AA, you never know just where the help will come from or who will deliver it.

Chris K. describes in his story "Hope in the Yard" how he was walking to the rec yard one day and happened to see a prisoner with some Grapevines in his hand. From this random encounter they began to talk, and before long "He became my sponsor," says Chris.

And, as sometimes happens in AA, the connection between one alcoholic and another can occur without the parties ever even meeting each other. "I got a sponsor through the AA correspondence program," says Tod C. in "From 3000 Miles Away." "He was nothing like me.... But what he was was an alcoholic, and one who had stayed sober for many years.... I never saw his face nor heard his voice, but he taught me how to live a sober life."

Of course, AA in prison is not without challenges and sometimes prison rules can present obstacles for outside volunteers coming in to serve as sponsors. But solutions can be found, as Karen C. discovered in her story "Planting Seeds." Working with the prison administrators at San Quentin, a pilot program got started, and "Now, many months later," says Karen, "we have over 60 AA members confined in San Quentin who have or are in the process of getting outside sponsorship."

Working the program with a sponsor can be one of the most effective ways of staying sober—in prison or on the outside. Speaking about the sponsor he got connected with through AA's Corrections Correspondence Service, Dan S. shares in "The Visitor," "Jeff and I are intimately connected, bonded by our similarities, not separated by our differences." And, after five years of sharing together by mail, Jeff traveled 1,400 miles across the country to meet with Dan in person in prison. "It was my first visit from anyone in 11 years," says Dan.

Hope in the Yard
July 2012

I n March of 2009, I woke up from a blackout in a place that was becoming all too familiar to me—the county jail. I came to my senses as the judge was advising me that the crime I was charged with carried a possible life sentence, and that she was setting my bail at $50,000. Fear gripped every fiber of my body.

At that point I barely had any clue what had happened the night the crime was committed. I vaguely remembered the week prior to the arrest. But I did have a foggy recollection of bawling my eyes out on the floor of the motel room I was living in and asking God to make it all stop. I was too scared to kill myself, but I was also too scared to go on. It wasn't dying I was afraid of. It was living.

My prayers were answered. As I woke up in the courtroom on March 16, 2009, I remembered what I had heard about being "careful what you pray for; it just might come true." I was feeling a rollercoaster of emotions as I sobered up. Mainly I was terrified of my future, yet so relieved that all the madness had stopped.

I stayed in the county jail for six months, as I went back and forth to court. I attended AA meetings brought into the jail, and I had a Big Book and a subscription to Grapevine. The original charge was reduced but, because of my prior record, I was sentenced to prison. I wasn't thrilled by the idea of doing time, but I know today it was part of a much bigger plan.

After sentencing, I wound up at a prison in North Florida that didn't offer AA meetings. One Saturday afternoon, as I was walking to the rec yard, I saw an inmate with some Grapevines in his hand. I knew I needed to talk to him. I went and introduced myself and asked him if he would like to read the Big Book with me sometime. We talked for three hours that day.

He explained that he was carrying Grapevines to a friend, and that he had published an article in the July 2009 prison issue ("Someone to Help," by Dirk S.) At that moment it dawned on me that he was there to help me, and I was there to help him. He became my sponsor.

That day we discussed the first three Steps, and he gave me instructions for working the Fourth Step, just as it is laid out in the Big Book. Within a few days I had completed it. We set a time for him to hear my Fifth Step. The following afternoon we headed out to the rec yard to do so. When I was done telling him my whole life story, the feeling was absolutely amazing! I felt freer on that rec yard than I have ever felt in my entire life.

From that moment on I was on fire for AA. Dirk was nearing the end of his sentence and soon went home, back to New York. I went home two months later, with a whole new zeal for AA. In the past, when I had tried the program, I didn't get to know anyone, and I surely did not let anyone get to know me. Needless to say, I always got drunk. I couldn't string together more than 30 days. The obsession to drink ruled me. This time—without a doubt—it was different.

The day I got out of prison I went to a meeting. I was looking for a guy who I had met on one of my many trips in and out of the rooms. I showed up at a meeting I thought he might be at; sure enough he was there. I asked him to be my sponsor. He said yes, and we wasted no time getting back into the Big Book. I became a student of the Big Book and a carrier of AA's message.

Around the time of my first month out of prison, I was approaching a year sober. The thought occurred to me that not only was I free from prison, I was also free from that terrible obsession that used to consume all my waking thoughts. I was starting to understand what happy, joyous and free meant. Life was finally worth living.

I got involved with a group of guys who are extremely active in their sobriety. They also have a lot of fun. We decided to take a road trip to Texas for the International Convention. The 18-hour car ride was a blast. As we got closer to San Antonio, the atmosphere was indescribably wonderful. As we were walking out of the registration area of the convention center, I couldn't believe my eyes: There was Dirk, my sponsor from prison! Not that long ago I would have looked at that whole situation as just one big coincidence. Now I know that I have an awakened spirit because I can see that it was no coincidence, but the loving hand of God.

Today my life is incredible. I truly have a life beyond my wildest dreams. As I sit here tonight, I am filled with gratitude. Tomorrow I will celebrate two years of sobriety. I have the love and respect of my family. I have a girlfriend who has never seen what a monster I can be when I drink. I have more true friends than I can count with both hands. I'm sponsoring two guys who I get to watch grow in this program. Guys like me don't get to enjoy these things.

If I had gotten what I deserved, I would be dead, or in prison for a long time. But that's not the case at all. I am a sober member of AA, and I am a free man. I am free from the bondage of self; I am free from the awful obsession to drink.

Chris K.
New Port Richey, Florida

Dear Manuel
July 2017

In 2000, I walked into my first AA meeting, beaten and completely defeated. I eventually got a sponsor, and it was suggested that I get into service.

At first, this meant chairing meetings. After that, I served as treasurer, GSR and several positions in my district. I also worked on local committees and helped out at AA assemblies and conventions. I did all these things because I didn't want to drink again. Yet I found myself longing for something different. I was soon to find it.

One day as I was getting my mail, I saw my monthly Grapevine in its little black plastic envelope. I always get excited when a new issue arrives. I opened it up and saw that it was the annual prison issue. I read it feverishly. I came across an article from a guy in jail telling of his gratitude to have a sponsor writing him from the outside.

This was it! This was just what I had been seeking—Corrections Correspondence—writing to alcoholics in jail. So I contacted the General Service Office (GSO) and it wasn't long before I got my first inmate to correspond with.

Back when I was first getting sober, it was suggested that I journal my feelings. I began to notice that I enjoyed writing. It became a special time with just God and me. Writing is a sort of like meditation. It helps me clarify things. One of the ways God has blessed me with my writing in sobriety is through this kind of correspondence. Writing to inmates is a real gift. And one of the wonderful surprises has been my friend Manuel.

Manuel and I have been writing each other for several years now. I actually requested and received three other inmate correspondents over the years, but they just wrote a couple of times and then dropped off. But Manuel and I have had a long, wonderful journey together. When he writes, his words leave the page with a positive resolve to change. His spirituality inspires me as he writes about helping other men in prison to find their way through the constant negative forces that surround them. "It would be easier to just give in to all that goes on in here," Manuel wrote. Yet he remains a strong, spiritual man. He truly believes that God has ordained this journey for him.

If life were truly fair, I would be where Manuel is, and be well-deserving of the accommodations. I've known people (both in and out of the program) and have read many stories in Grapevine over the years of alcoholics who, while driving drunk, have killed someone. I drove for more than 30 years (sometimes with my family aboard) legally drunk. I can never speak of the unfairness of life, not with what God has done for me. Manuel and I both agree that God has a plan for everything and everyone, at every moment.

For some reason, I didn't have such a hard landing. I guess I owe this one to God. One take-away from my experience with Manuel is that perhaps I was spared so that I can help carry the message of AA. Manuel and I have corresponded on this subject. He too is in a position to carry the message, even in prison. He and I both feel God put us together. My job is to share my experience, strength and hope with Manuel, and he will share his with others. Hope is what we talk about in our letters.

Fortunately, Manuel was recently transferred to a better facility that has many recovery programs, ones designed to rehabilitate and move him closer to a release date.

I don't know what I am doing for Manuel's well-being, but I do know full well what he has done for me. He has taught me about life. His strength to endure, to want to change, to be the person God designed him to be, has impressed me immensely.

Sometimes I question my own strength and hope when I compare myself to where he is. But isn't that what God has planned all along? I, who have everything—a house, car, job—get to learn gratitude from an inmate who has "three hots and a cot."

And he can learn from me. He knows that just because I am free in this world and have a little bit of financial stability, doesn't preclude me from doing time in the prison of a "self-deluded" mind. I can (and have) felt life wasn't fair, and in the final days of my alcoholism, welcomed prison, and even death, rather than have to deal with the depression and mind-numbing despair of not being able to make a choice about whether to drink.

Contacting GSO to do Corrections Correspondence Service was one of the best decisions I've made since I put the cork in the jug nine years ago. And finding a spiritual pen pal in Manuel is just another gift from AA and my Higher Power. I've been taught freedom from a man behind bars. Life will inevitably continue to challenge me. It happens. But along with challenges come great rewards.

If I ever think (and of course I undoubtedly will at some point) that I've got it bad, that life just isn't living up to my expectations, I just have to pick up my pen and write Manuel. Someday, I hope to meet him on the outside, a free man.

Matt S.
Buffalo Grove, Illinois

From 3000 Miles Away

June 2015

From my first drink at 12 years old, I kept going until I got sick and passed out. This seemed perfectly normal to me, since this is pretty much how I saw my parents do it. In high school I began to mix other things with my alcohol, but I remained an alcoholic at heart. As much as I hated to admit it, I had become like my father. I began to commit felonies to support my addictions, and prison sentences followed. Finally, at 35 years old, I was sentenced to 30 years to life. As a "career criminal," society had given up on me, and I had given up hope on myself.

I sobered up many times over the years, sometimes voluntarily and sometimes not. I had many opportunities to change the course of my life, but I refused to look within myself and see that the problem was not simply the alcohol and drugs.

Finally, at eight years into my life sentence and deep in my alcoholism, I reached a point where I could not go on. So late one night in my prison cell, I decided to end my life. I made a plan I was sure would succeed, but now I look back and see how a Higher Power saved me. The medical professionals brought me back to life.

When I woke, I found myself in a rubber room on suicide watch. It was then I finally realized my actions were hurting all those who loved me. I could no longer tell myself the lie that I was only harming myself. I knew that alcohol was no longer the answer, but wasn't sure how I was going to stop. Still, I had to put myself through the wringer one more time. A few months later, I went on a three-day bender, but found no relief at all. I was then put on a bus and transferred to another prison. I thought this a horrible turn of events. But it ended up being exactly what I needed, just like that trip to the rubber room.

When I arrived at my new "home," I did the traditional meet with the homeboys and I passed inspection. I told them I no longer drank or used and would appreciate it if they did not include me in any way in these activities. To this day I have no idea why I said this, for I had never done so in the past. Besides, after my recent bender, I had no real reason to believe I'd actually follow through. But after our "meeting" was over, one of the homeboys, Bruce R., invited me to another sort of meeting—a meeting of Alcoholics Anonymous. Again, without even thinking, I said yes. That was March 3, 2004, and from that day to this, I have remained sober.

I got a sponsor through the AA correspondence program. His name was Jim P., and he was nothing like me. He had never spent a day in jail, never done a drug and he was gay. But what he was was an alcoholic, and one who had stayed sober for many years. From 3,000 miles away, he walked me through the Steps. I never saw his face nor heard his voice, but he taught me how to live a sober life.

I began to look within myself and to take responsibility for my actions, something I was always so horribly frightened of. I did those Fourth and Fifth Steps, which I thought would be impossible. I had a deep dark secret I had not shared with a single soul for 32 years; I was going to take it to the grave with me. But after working the first three Steps, my Higher Power gave me the strength to share my secret with Jim. I had been molested by a man when I was 12 (around the time I took that first drink), and I thought what had happened to me that day was my fault. I carried that guilt for years. Jim told me that it was absolutely not my fault, and that it didn't change who I was as a person, or how he saw me. A huge weight was lifted.

Since then I have shared that "secret" with all of my sponsees, and even in a couple of meetings. Letting it out into the light of day has freed me from the power it had over me. I share it because it helps me, but also in the hope that it will help others.

I've been sober almost 11 years now, and Jim has since passed away, but he gave me so much. I owe him a debt no amount of money could possibly repay. He was the most patient and caring man I ever met. He wrote me faithfully almost every single week for seven years straight.

He was a gift from my HP. As hard as it was to move on, I have gotten another sponsor and he's teaching me even more. I have learned that my alcoholism wasn't just about my drinking. I didn't know how to deal with reality, and I wasn't comfortable in my own skin. I had no idea who Tod was. I was full of fear and I was trying to cover it all up with a tough "convict" exterior.

Since working through the Steps several times and applying them in my daily life, attending many meetings and sponsoring others, I've become pretty comfortable with myself. I'm OK with Tod today. I no longer have to put something in my body to change how I feel. Whatever feelings I have, they will pass. Today I don't drink or use no matter what.

I've been in here 19 years now, and I still have about 10 more before I go to the parole board, but my life is not about the day I'm released. I get up each morning and I ask my HP to give me the strength to stay sober one more day, to show me how to be of service, and to help me see what I can give, rather than what I can get. I sponsor five guys, and the feeling I get from helping them is so much better than any high I've ever known. People actually like me and trust me. People even seek me out for advice, and I'm sometimes told what a good guy I am. That's crazy!

My grown sons talk to me and tell me they love me. Their mom even talks to me from time to time, and she treats me with respect. I've met a wonderful woman who loves me and wants to marry me. She tells me I'm the best thing that has ever happened to her. I am now capable of loving her back and treating her like the special person she is.

I no longer feel like it's me against the world, and I'm now able to accept others, character defects and all. We are all flawed and make mistakes, myself included, and I'm even learning to accept that too. I no longer lie down at night hoping I won't wake up. Often I'm full of joy and peace. All these gifts and much more are because of AA and my HP. Today I have a purpose, and that's to carry the message. If you are an alcoholic like me, I pray you too can find freedom and a happy and joyous sober life.

Tod C.
Chino, California

Something Positive

July 2019

You might think staying sober in prison should be easy, right? It's not. Sometimes, I think it may be even harder to stay sober in here than out there, but then I remember how hard it was out there too.

By the grace of God, I celebrated my one-year anniversary in December. It's sad to say, but that was not the day I was incarcerated. In prison, I had to bump my head (literally) a couple of times before I realized how powerless I am. I know I need to change or I may just wind up in here again, if I'm lucky enough not to die beforehand. I'm afraid that my bottom would be death.

So a year ago I made a decision that I would at least give the AA program a proper try. I used to go to AA sporadically in the outside world and I loved it. At the same time, I also loved living life on my terms instead of God's (or AA's) terms. Now, I put as much effort into my recovery as I did into getting drunk or high.

For the first time, I have a sponsor who I met through the Correctional Facilities Committee, who I correspond with. I am working through the Steps with my sponsor, instead of doing them myself, like I used to.

We are now on the Fourth Step and I am trying to be as thorough as possible, even though the work can be pretty daunting at times. I keep my daily reprieve by reading the Big Book and "Twelve and Twelve" regularly, along with my *Daily Reflections* book.

Meetings are held in this prison only twice a month, so I'm also eternally grateful to Grapevine for getting me through the "in-betweens." My sponsor blessed me with a subscription and gave me my other AA books, so I'm pretty well-equipped to deal with the very toxic environment in here.

Staying sober in here is really hard. I'm one of the few guys trying to do something positive and better myself. I try to remember that maybe, by my example, I might be able to help other alcoholics in here who are suffering. Just about everybody is living one day at a time in here, so I might just have some ground to work with. Until then, I keep sober, keep coming back, keep it simple and keep it real.

Benjamin Z.
Dilley, Texas

Planting Seeds

June 2020

Since 1987, one of the defining characteristics of my sobriety has been my participation in the NorCal (Northern California) Hospitals & Institutions (H & I) Committee. While I've loved all my service work, carrying the message of AA to the alcoholic who is confined has been the service commitment that matched perfectly with my particular mix of assets and defects, truly allowing me to be usefully whole in spite of myself.

Doing H & I service has taught me so many invaluable lessons—how to maintain singleness of purpose, how to be dependable (unlike on the outside, if I don't make it to an H & I meeting, there may not be a meeting), how to put the common welfare ahead of my own and how to express myself without dropping the f-bomb all over the room. It's also allowed me to use my God-given assets to serve others. From my beginnings as a foot-soldier volunteer at a local hospital to the honor of serving as the chair of the NorCal committee, carrying the message to the alcoholic who's confined has been one of the great blessings of my sobriety.

For many years, our committee has been challenged by our inability to provide sponsorship—that all-important element of recovery—to alcoholics confined in our many state prisons. Whenever I talk to a newcomer at an AA meeting I suggest, as was suggested to me: 1) get a Big Book; 2) go to meetings; and 3) get a sponsor to work the Steps.

For decades since 1942, H & I committees have been successfully providing the first two elements—bringing in AA meetings and providing ample supplies of literature to members confined in state prisons. But due to conflicts with the Department of Corrections' regulations on program volunteers, we've been unable to crack that third vital element of sponsorship. Simply put, the California Department of Corrections and Rehabilitation (CDCR) classifies AA volunteers as unpaid or free staff who, as such, need to comply with all rules and regulations of regular staff. One of the predominant (and logical) rules is that staff aren't allowed to engage in "overfamiliarity" with prisoners.

Well, overfamiliarity is practically the definition of sponsorship. So how we can provide that without breaking the rules of the prison, and thus endangering our entire efforts, has been our ongoing and perplexing dilemma.

One evening, I came home from a meeting where I'd given a newcomer my usual spiel about the three things she could do to help ensure her sobriety, and I began surfing the CDCR website "looking for loopholes" in their regulations. Annoyingly, a link for how to visit prisoners kept coming up, and I kept dismissing it (much like 33 years ago, I had dismissed so many other of God's attempts to help me). Yet inadvertently, I ended up clicking on the link.

After softly hurling a few profanities at my computer, I actually looked at the page, which read:

"VISITING A FRIEND OR LOVED ONE IN PRISON—Visits from family and friends keep inmates socially connected, which helps in their rehabilitation."

Uh-huh. Wait a minute...isn't that what we're trying to be—AA friends? Suddenly, a lightbulb went on and I realized we'd been coming at this from entirely the wrong direction.

So the committee tried a new approach: If we enter the prison through the "visiting" department simply as "friends" rather than entering the prison through the Adult Services Program as "program volunteers," it might eliminate the obstacles. No more need for certain compliances and 26-page clearance forms. Eureka! For us to do this we needed an entirely separate roster of volunteers, one in which sponsorship experience rather than specific H & I experience was the main criteria.

I immediately called a few committee members just to make sure this wasn't a case of early onset dementia. Sometimes simple solutions are frightening in their blatant obviousness. But after examining the idea from all angles, we decided it might be worth pursuing.

In 2018, we began developing a pilot program. We defined the program, wrote position descriptions, and decided that San Quentin would be the best place to test our new endeavor. We began meeting with the prison administration and presented our idea, showing the many potential benefits to both the prisoners and to the prison.

We got the administration's wholehearted support, but our biggest logistical challenge was anonymity. We had to draw a line in the sand on that, because we had to protect our volunteers' anonymity. And because we'd done the solid footwork, the warden was so convinced of our potential that he allowed us to customize the simple one-page visitor clearance form so that it red-flags our visitor applications and the last names of our visitors are never shared with prisoners.

Our committee held meetings, conducted thorough orientations and fielded questions. We also got a dedicated post office box. We designed a flyer/application to inform the prisoners of the opportunity for outside sponsorship.

Every morning, I asked God to give me inspiration, an intuitive thought or decision, to give me a clue that this was God's will, not mine. All I can say is that although there have definitely been bumps in the road, with every new development we seemed to move forward. In late March of 2019, we paired our first volunteer with a sponsee and have been operational ever since. Now, many months later, we have over 60 AA members confined in San Quentin who have or are in the process of getting outside sponsorship. Imagine the potential over time at prisons across the country.

Yes, it's taken a lot of time and energy, but whenever I feel like slacking, I have to ask myself...Would I be sober today without sponsorship? What if all I'd been able to do in AA was go to meetings and read the literature? To those volunteers who have been willing to participate in our groundbreaking effort of a pilot program, who have participated in the "flying blind" stages of this solution, I cannot sufficiently express my enormous gratitude. So perhaps the best way to end is to share some of their experience, strength and hope.

One volunteer, with 34 years of sobriety, told us, "It's one of the best Twelfth Step experiences of my sobriety." Another said, "The internal network of San Quentin sponsees is getting stronger and stronger. We're witnessing the Fellowship grow and grow. I'm so blessed to serve and sponsor in this program." And another said, "When my inside sponsee shared his list of fears with me, I was humbled in a way that I never have been before while hearing a Fifth Step. His fears made every other list of fears I've heard—my own included—seem completely ridiculous."

One of the prisoners in the sponsorship program said, "I and others feel that we can finally be honest and share all parts of our lives during a Fourth Step. Having to hold back information from inmate sponsors has affected us. I now feel that I will be able to trust someone." Another inmate said, "I'm looking forward to my first visit in 30 years, but mostly I'm looking forward to working all the Steps." And finally, one prisoner wrote the committee to say, "I'm writing to let you know you've been approved to visit me. I haven't had a visitor in 10 years. I can't wait to meet you. I need a lot of help."

Karen C.
Oakland, California

Someday, Coffee and Honey Buns
July 2014

'm writing this from a Florida prison, where it's hard to get to an AA meeting. When I first got in here in 2010, we had meetings; I actually used to chair them for a while. I also used to chair meetings on the outside.

The meeting we had here was good. It was held in a small classroom near the recovery program area. I was there on a daily basis and really got into recovery. I also wrote to the AA World Services office about the Corrections Correspondence Program, and I got an outside AA sponsor who helped me work the Steps.

I made some good friends at our meeting. It got big and had to be expanded and moved into the visitation area. An outside sponsor came in twice a month. We had some good times there. A lot of inmates attended. We had chairmen, service positions and good staff support—everything except coffee, which would have come in handy the day a couple of guys took a bunch of honey buns out of the vending machines.

Our meeting also had an AA library with books sent from World Services. They helped us out a lot. In prison, AA meetings take a lot of work. We had to take attendance, set up chairs and put out flyers in all the dorms. It was hard to do all of this because of all the security procedures here. We also had a chaplain who came in once a month and talked about the car dealership he used to own. I liked his stories. I worked in a dealership too.

Now the meeting is gone and so is the recovery program. I still have my AA sponsor, Max. I have my daily meditation books and my subscription to Grapevine—thanks to Max. I read the Big Book every day. That's like having Bill W. and Dr. Bob in the room with you.

This is how I stay sober on the inside. Sometimes in recovery you have to think outside the box. Maybe we will get another AA meeting. I hope so.

Dave S.
Graceville, Florida

End Run
July 2018

When I walked into the bank and handed the teller a note demanding money, all I cared about was making it to the bar a few blocks away. Later, as my photo appeared on the noon news report broadcasting on the television above the shot glasses, I hoped nobody would recognize me.

The next day, I drank myself right up to the sheriff's office and turned myself in, thinking they would go easy on me.

Sitting in the small jail cell, waiting to be sentenced, I didn't see any alcohol or drugs, but the stories I heard there of life in federal prison helped me envision my next five years as a comfortable buzz.

My first impression of the penitentiary in Texas was that the place was completely unruly and the people there were insane. The place was filled with drugs and alcohol and violence. It looked like a big, dangerous party with everyone drinking and getting high.

Looking back, I know that it was my Higher Power that stepped in and sent a guy named Skyler to meet me on my first day in the yard. Out of the 1,200 men on the compound, few were looking for sobriety and none were as dedicated to AA and helping others as Skyler.

I had spent 20 years as a drunk, destroying myself and every relationship that mattered. As Skyler and I talked during a lap around the track in the prison yard one day, I knew that I wanted what he had.

I had taken up space at AA meetings on the street to get my probation papers signed for courts, but I never gave AA a real chance. I had never worked the Steps and I had huge issues with the existence of a Higher Power.

In prison, Skyler became my sponsor and got me working the Steps and going to meetings three times a week. It was a small meeting of about eight people, but they were all devoted to helping me and each other.

After almost a year, I finally finished my Fourth Step and it was the most amazing feeling I ever had. All that baggage that I carried around for years no longer held me down. My excuses to drink were gone. I finally felt free.

When Skyler completed his time and went home, I took over the AA meetings and started helping other men work the Steps. I wrote GSO about AA Correspondence and began writing to a member named Bill H. He got me a subscription to Grapevine and I started a Sunday morning Grapevine meeting in our prison. It's a huge success now; we have about 15 guys some days.

I began spending my time working on my Ninth Step. I wrote letters of amends to try and heal the relationships I had damaged in my family.

Christmas just went by and I can honestly say it was the best holiday season I've had in years. I now have over two years of sobriety and I feel really good about myself. It says in the Big Book that, "We have found much of heaven and we have been rocketed into a fourth dimension of existence of which we have not even dreamed." I have taken a small ride on that rocket since I've been working the program here in this prison and I am so looking forward to sobriety on the outside.

Charles H.
Atwater, California

The Visitor

July 2017

It's humbling to admit that prison saved my life. Every day of sobriety that has been given to me has occurred behind these walls. AA is responsible for this miracle.

Trusting the Twelve Step process was not easy for me. My false ego and defiant attitude fought the solution for half of my 21 years of continuous incarceration here. Finally despair and humiliation broke my self-will into shards of hopelessness and I cried out and asked for help.

I have now experienced what I call a gentle spiritual awakening. I have spiritual principles now, which are trustworthy, proven and enduring. I truly believe they are given to us once we surrender to our Higher Power. AA is my map for living.

Today, I'm connected to God, others and myself. I have been able to restore many of my relationships and have developed new ones because I can be interested in the well-being of others. I deeply appreciate the AA angels who do Hospital & Institutions service. They carry the seeds of hope into these places of isolation.

In 2007, I was lucky enough to be connected to a kind and caring human being via the AA Corrections Correspondence Service (CCS). The man's name is Jeff S. He's a sober AA member. He has become a significant part of my recovery and journey.

Jeff and I are intimately connected, bonded by our similarities, not separated by our differences. We openly exchange our ideas, challenges and experiences. He lives in a rural community in the upper midwest. I'm out on the west coast, physically in prison. But spiritually, our energies connect, transcending the distance and physical barriers between us.

AA is a program filled with the wonder of paradox. For example, we only keep what we have by giving it away. This dramatic shift in my consciousness fills me with humility and grace and continues to stretch me as a spiritual being. Jeff understands this concept.

Jeff has shared how he once lived in his own internal prison. Our fellowship shows that prison has no boundaries. Writing Jeff letters from a prison cell with a spirit of freedom and gratitude is heartwarming. Furthermore, he teaches me lessons about acceptance. I struggled for years with self-acceptance. I have punished myself more than anyone else can because I killed an innocent human being.

Through the process of taking responsibility, and a life of amends and working at letting go of punishing myself, I have gained the tools to become a better person and live in the stream of life. Jeff's example and experience has resonated with me. He has taught me that acceptance is not just an ending, but a beginning. When I secretly wouldn't accept myself, he did. His caring spirit extended across the plains to me. He has "walked" with me as I grew in the Fellowship. I'm connected to another sober human being.

One day in 2012, a milestone occurred in my AA journey. Jeff came all the way out west and met me inside this California prison where I'm incarcerated. After five years of sharing our experience, strength and hope in letters, we now sat face-to-face. He traveled 1,400 miles one way to meet with another alcoholic. It was my first visit from anyone in 11 years.

That afternoon, Jeff and I had lunch and we shared our memories, our sobriety and our joy. He had talked about this day for more than two years. He carried the AA message across the country in a selfless act of service. His example has forever touched my heart and spirit. Thank you, AA.

Dan S.
Soledad, California

17 Years of Hope
June 2020

I attended my first AA meeting in 1981 in Alhambra, California. It was a blessing. I was 19.

I'm writing to share my gratitude about being able to carry the AA message and my experience, strength and hope to another woman who's incarcerated. My friend in prison had a sentence of 15 to 30 years. She's a bit older and sober several years more than me. Pretty darn amazing. The General Service Office in New York sent me her address during her first year in prison. That was more than 17 years ago.

So for these many years, our letters have traveled back and forth from an old farmhouse in rural Kansas to a mega state prison in Arizona. We've discussed Steps, resentments, solutions, Traditions, bills, goals, the Slogans and God. We've sometimes even discussed making desserts.

Sentiments of love are exchanged, as we pass letters about the lighter and harder parts of life in sobriety...things like the death of family members, running over the dog, making my first cheesecake, not getting to enough meetings, getting fatter, getting thinner, getting beaten up by a cell mate—and the valuable lesson of easy does it.

AA taught me that action helps me stay sober. For the two of us, action is picking up a pen, getting paper and a stamp and writing an address on an envelope. For her, pens, paper, stamps and envelopes are luxuries. They are not easy to get.

One day at a time, she and I have racked up a lot of postage miles in these 17 years. Because she has more sobriety, she has often sponsored me toward a fresher perspective and greater serenity as we trudge this road. Yes, it's possible to walk, talk and write the path of sobriety from the "inside"-out through the mail. It's been one of the most endearing trips in sobriety I have ever taken.

Tess M.
Kansas

6

Carrying the Message

E motional change usually comes from the inside out, but in the case of the AA members in this chapter, it can also come from the outside in—in the form of carrying the message in behind the walls. It's a very special kind of service in AA—a service that truly cuts both ways: helping the members on the inside just as much as the members on the outside.

The story "Mary in Folsom" shares the experience of an outside AA who has been carrying the message behind the walls and growing because of it. "I've often wondered," Mary says of her many conversations with members on the inside, "how they stay sober in there with all the temptation and boredom they have to face. But then, they ask me how I can stay sober out here with all the temptations and distractions I have." It helps Mary to see that the program of AA and its Steps and Traditions "are all an internal journey."

That journey crosses many boundaries, where people from totally different backgrounds intersect with a single purpose: to carry the AA message of hope and recovery to another alcoholic. "For the hour and a half, I'm there," says Sara S. in "We're in This Together," "we are simply human beings. We are fellow alcoholics. We are mothers, sisters, daughters, all sharing in the glorious, tragic, heartbreaking, miraculous experience of our common struggle."

It's hard to know where the journey of sobriety will lead, but for one Canadian AA member carrying the message to an Aboriginal man in a jail cell in Canberra, Australia provided an opportunity for growth—

from the inside out: "As a firefighter I had to be prepared to rush into burning buildings, but I had been afraid to take the AA message into jail." Having built a protective wall around himself, says John K., "The first real crack in that wall was made sitting in that small white room with that man in the Canberra jail."

For the AAs in this chapter, carrying the message is a journey that never ends.

Mary in Folsom

July 2018

I'm one of the lucky AA members who get to go into Folsom Prison to participate in an AA meeting with the prisoners. I get to go once a month and it's the highlight of my month.

The meeting takes place in a "Level 4" facility. Level 4 is for prisoners who are considered the most dangerous, and yet I never feel afraid in there. The guys I've come to know are men who are growing and living their lives to the best of their abilities under very trying circumstances. They are not the gangsters they might have once been. Many of them were sentenced many years ago for crimes they committed when they were teenagers. I don't know what crimes they are incarcerated for, and I don't want to know. I know who they are now and that's enough for me.

During these prison meetings, we have tackled difficult problems, such as how does one make amends to the family of someone you killed or someone whose death you were involved in? Then there are questions about living in prison, such as how does one live a life relatively free of resentments, when every day you are confronted by irrational demands and provocation? Or, how does one resist temptation when drugs or alcohol are available almost daily, and when the culture behind the walls says that something is wrong with you if you are sober?

In the years I've been going into Folsom, I have lost friends to stabbings, relocation and sometimes even promotion to Level 3 prisons. I miss each and every one of the guys I've come to know. These guys also get to know me.

I was never in prison, or even in jail. I don't have to have those same experiences to relate with alcoholism. Yet I've learned how to stay sober and find joy in life. It doesn't matter where I am. My internal life matters in sobriety. When I walk into a meeting at Folsom, the guys who know me know I love and accept them as they are. What they don't know is how much I carry them with me all month. I've come to love and respect the journeys they have to walk.

I've often wondered how they stay sober in there with all the temptation and boredom they have to face. But then, they ask me how I can stay sober out here with all the temptation and distractions I have.

I am reminded once again that the program of AA and its Steps and Traditions are all an internal journey. And how lucky we are to be on this road.

Mary
Grass Valley, California

The Hate-and-Pain Guy

July 2002

The other day I was trying to remember what the actual turning point for me in the program was. I think it was when I really started to get into service work, and, specifically, taking meetings into institutions.

The first time I went into a prison was when this oldtimer, Vic, invited me to go with a group of guys from my home group to a meeting at Sheridan Federal Prison. I was really surprised at how good an AA meeting it was. I mean, there was a clear topic, everyone seemed to take it pretty seriously, all the guys seemed to be well-versed in the program, and I got a lot out of everyone's talks. I probably was the only weak link in the whole thing. With two years sober, I was one of the newest guys to AA at that meeting. Since most of the guys in Sheridan were doing pretty long stretches of time, and a lot of the guys started going to AA not too long after they got in, several of them had five to 10 years of sobriety. And I thought I was going to be schooling the poor inmates on how to stay sober. Man, I had a lot to learn.

Every meeting I went to, I gained more respect for the guys in that group. They had their own secretary and chairperson. They were sponsoring each other and going through the Steps. I also found out that inmates going to an AA meeting in a federal prison weren't real popular. I guess it made the guys suspect you of being a narc. If you were trying to change your life for the better, and in the process you were refusing to drink any homemade pruno or to take any yard drugs, all the other inmates thought you might be the kind of guy who would rat them out. So a lot of the guys were walking the yard pretty much alone. Yet they still came. And they taught me so much. I tried to show them that a guy could stay sober out on the streets, and they showed me how to live an honorable life even in a place where you were considered just a number.

I started to go in pretty regularly with my buddy George, who was the Oregon area coordinator for Sheridan. That was until George started to get very ill and the meetings at the prison began to fall off. George ended up in the hospital with cancer and end-stage diabetes a couple months later. I remember getting guilt-tripped by one of the guys in our group to go visit him in the hospital. Man, I hated hospitals—all those sick people. But I went, and there was George in the cancer ward with his foot half amputated, given only a month or so to live. Angel (a friend of ours who helped start the AA meetings out at Sheridan from the inside, and who had since gotten out and become a big part of our local AA community) was also there visiting George. It was all a bit too gloomy for my taste.

George proceeded to deliver a classic deathbed request. He asked me if I would take over for him as the coordinator for Sheridan. He went into a long, moving speech about how it had been his life's work for the past eight years, how I was the only one who really knew the clearance system, and how it would put his heart at ease to know that someone who really cared was taking it over for him. Of course, I fell for it, not being nearly as savvy as I had thought I was. They both started laughing hysterically. Even worse was bumping into the shift nurse as I was leaving and hearing her say that George got visitors all day long, that there was constant laughter coming from his room, and that he was the only patient they could remember on the cancer ward who laughed so much. Well, George finally passed away, laughing to the very end, and I ended up taking a couple of meetings a month into Sheridan.

It took me a while to get the hang of this new service commitment, but I really enjoyed the meetings out at the prison. Oh, and there was that other little benefit: I hadn't taken a drink in quite some time. I became pretty good friends with most of the regulars at the meeting, and I could spot a new guy a mile away. One in particular, Garvar, began to catch my attention. He was a real muscular guy with tattoos from head to toe (not that that really distinguished him in the joint). He was very quiet and seemed to have a constant undercurrent of anger about him. But he seemed really serious about the program and was always very attentive at the meetings. Even though he wasn't all that social a guy at the beginning, we seemed to hit it off right from the start. As time went on, Garv (or the Hate-and-Pain Guy, as some volunteers at first called him because he had "hate" and "pain" tattooed across his knuckles) began to loosen up in the meetings and became a real part of the home group.

A couple of years went by, and Garv was about to get out of prison. To my surprise, he decided to relocate to the Eugene area, as Angel had some five years back. I guess that because he had gotten to know several of us volunteers from the Eugene area, he felt it would be better to hang with us rather than with his old running buddies back in L.A. I soon was bumping into him around town at the meetings the halfway house let him attend. A few months later, he was out altogether.

Garv eventually asked me to sponsor him, and I agreed with some reservations. I had sponsored guys before, but no one with his sort of background and years in the joint. So I was a bit concerned that we wouldn't be able to relate about those issues. I thought maybe he should look for someone who had done some time in prison to sponsor him. But we figured if it wasn't working out, he could find someone else down the road.

At the beginning, Garv was real uncomfortable on the outside.

There were all these new personalities to deal with. And worse yet, there were all these damn details of life—driver's license, rent, taxes, all sorts of applications. I don't think either of us were sure he was going to make it. I think he thought more about doing some kind of crime to get put back into prison rather than drinking. Certainly, the thought of escape from reality popped up from time to time. So I told Garv that the only thing that worked for me when I got thirsty was to work with others. By this time, I had been elected the Hospitals and Institutions chair for our local intergroup, so I had lots of connections with different facilities around town. Garv and I started hitting a bunch of different meetings in treatment centers and detoxes, and things got a bit better—but not a whole lot.

Then one day, I got a call from the coordinator of a halfway house for youth offenders. He said that no volunteers would come in anymore, because the last time they took a meeting into the kids, the kids all started throwing the Big Books back at them. He said that it was nearly impossible to hold a meeting for these kids who were mandated by the facility to go, because they constantly acted out. He recommended that we discontinue the meeting. I told him I thought I might have someone I could bring to the meeting whom they probably wouldn't throw Big Books at, and maybe we should give it one more try.

So off to the halfway house Garv and I went. Now, I knew that none of these kids were going to mess with Garv, but I doubted that either of us was going to have much of an impact on any of these juvenile delinquents. I couldn't have been more wrong. They took to Garv like bees to honey. Acting tough around Garv just didn't make sense, and those kids knew it. He had been every place they had been and probably every place they might be going to. And he had this incredible way with them. He knew the pecking order of the kids right away and could win over the top dog in a matter of minutes. And in the cases where a kid, no way, no how, was going to go along with Garv, he could put him in his place and pretty much eliminate his influence on the rest of the group. Those kids actually started to look forward to the weekly AA meetings, because that's when Garvar was coming. He began to sponsor half the little hoodlums. The facility even gave him permission to take the kids out for meetings and movies and stuff in the evenings. He seemed to be the only one at the time who was really getting through to these kids, so everyone wanted him as involved with their recovery as possible.

All these developments started having an incredible effect on the rest of Garv's life. In a short amount of time, he was asked to become a live-in house president for one of the larger recovery houses in town. He also decided that youth counseling was the direction in which he wanted to go as a career, so he applied for grants and loans and registered for college. Up until then, he had been working in manual labor jobs like roofing and landscaping because those were the only jobs he could get so soon out of prison. He figured he had nothing to lose by becoming a full-time student. He eventually started taking meetings into the lock-down treatment center attached to the youth jail in town, and the results were pretty much the same. He seemed to have the gift with any group of young men he worked with.

I tagged along with him to these different youth meetings for about eight months or so, but eventually burned out on those types of facilities. I just didn't have the patience needed for those groups of kids. But I really did enjoy watching Garv work with them. It has been one of the highlights of my sobriety.

After about a year of taking the meeting into the youth treatment facility and going to college, Garv got offered an entry-level counseling job there. And probably not more than a year later, the after-care counseling position opened up. The problem for Garv was that the position required a bachelor's degree or equivalent experience in the field. But Garv figured what the heck, and put in for it anyway. It turned out that all the kids in the facility went into the director's office and told him that they wanted Garv to be their after-care counselor, and that was that. So here he was, just three years out of prison, with his own office, computer, and even business cards. Watching Garv hand out his business cards to some of his buddies at our home group had to be one of the prettiest sights I've ever seen.

One of the neatest things about these developments with Garv was that he became a hero for the guys still locked up in Sheridan. The first thing they wanted to hear about when I showed up was the latest news on Garv. A lot of the guys could remember Garv coming into the meeting and how angry he was. Hell, he was angry even for an inmate, let alone us sweet folks on the outside. Hearing stories about him becoming a professional and working with these kids was downright inspirational. They all started thinking they had a chance to make it on the outside. I'm telling you, hope can be pretty damn contagious.

Garv is still working as a counselor, and I'm still going into facilities. I really feel like H & I work is some of the purest Twelfth Step work out there these days. There's just not as many of those classic Twelfth Step calls of old. Most people find out about AA and recovery through treatment facilities, psych wards, or jails these days. In facilities, you get that rare chance to talk to someone who doesn't know anything about AA and desperately wants to get sober. It is a great feeling to let them know that there is a way out.

I'm not writing just to tell you some kind of fairy tale, though. We all know that there are no guarantees that Garv or I will stay sober. We both certainly have our good days and bad. But I do know that the incredible events that we have experienced in the program can never be taken away, not even with a drink. They happened, and no one can say this thing doesn't work.

I remember my sponsor, Jack, giving me a pep talk some time ago when I was all bummed out about the progress of a sponsee I had. He told me that all you can do is tell him what worked for you. The rest is up to him and God. And every once in a while, the guy "gets it" and then you get a front-row seat to the miracle.

Harold B.
Eugene, Oregon

We're In This Together

June 2020

I began earnestly looking for ways to be of service when I was six months sober. Soon, I heard that AA brought meetings into the county jail in my area and something clicked. I knew I wanted to do this. I had worked in a correctional facility shortly after nursing school and I understood some of the inner workings of the prison system. I had never been locked in, however. Somehow, I had escaped this misfortune, but only by the grace of God. And despite my initial attraction to the opportunity, I had apprehension as well. The unknown was intimidating. And yet...

The moment I sat down in that little jail library with those women, I felt the instant camaraderie and kinship that I feel whenever I enter an AA meeting anywhere. It did not matter that these women had committed crimes. Hadn't we all? If our crimes were not punishable by state law, they were certainly an offense to the heart, the mind and the spirit. Our guilt was the same, along with our fear of life without alcohol, our pain at the damage that we caused, our aimlessness, our longing, our loneliness.

These were the commonalities that I saw in the eyes of every woman sitting in that room. Like them, I had felt unlovable and ashamed. I also ached at the suffering I had caused my children. I too wanted a better life than the one afforded me by years of heavy drinking. And I had been in my own prison. My prison existed in a glass bottle, a flask, a ceramic mug that I kept perpetually filled under the sink in my bathroom. I knew hopelessness. And I had found a way out. The miracle is that I have found myself feeling more at home in that jail library than anywhere else.

Three years later, I still visit women in my county jail. They remind me of the prison I no longer have to live in. But they also give me hope.

They inspire me with their courage, honesty and willingness to be vulnerable. When I walk into that library and the doors lock behind me, I am never afraid. I'm among my people; I'm amid family.

For the hour and a half I'm there, we are simply human beings. We are fellow alcoholics. We are mothers, sisters, daughters, all sharing in the glorious, tragic, heartbreaking, miraculous experience of our common struggle. And during our brief time together, we share the hope for a brighter future.

Perhaps I'm able to help another alcoholic who's currently serving time behind bars by simply sharing my experience, strength and hope. I don't know. What I do know, is that those women continue to keep me sober, by sharing their lives with me.

Sara S.
Carbondale, Colorado

They Got to See the Best of Me
September 2015

I served nine stretches in jail before I found AA in my final incarceration. So I was glad when our area's corrections committee asked me to speak at what I thought was going to be an informational meeting for parolees in downtown St. Louis.

When I walked into the room however, I quickly realized things weren't what I had expected. There were no parolees there, just a large screen TV, a video camera and a few corrections officers.

I recognized one of the officers. She was associated with the prison in which I had finally found recovery through AA. When I had been in that prison, she told me that I was easily distracted. She noticed that I often went in too many directions and said I needed to "stay on course."

AA had helped me do that, and after my final release, I was able to go to the birthday party of my son. I had delivered and lost custody of him while I was incarcerated. At the party, I got a goodie bag that contained a little compass prize. That compass reminded me of what the officer had told me about staying on course. It also reminded me of our AA saying about "trudging the road" of happy destiny. I always had to look words up and I'd found that trudging meant to walk with purpose. I'd hung on to that compass ever since as a reminder.

Now that officer and I were together again. Many times, as I had passed in and out of the revolving doors of corrections institutions, I'd seen despair in the eyes of the people who tried to help me. But this time I saw tears of joy. She was so excited to see me sober. I cried too, grateful that she could finally see me a different way, as something other than a smart aleck con.

Now I was a sober member of AA, showing up to give back. I asked her about the video equipment and she explained that I was going to speak to women in a prison pre-release program at the very institution where I had been incarcerated. I just wanted to bawl.

After I got out of prison the last time and it was clear that I was sober through AA and that it would stick this time, I wanted to be able to serve people still in prison, but I really wanted to go back to the institution where I had served time. There were women there who didn't have the answer I now had. I felt that I could be uniquely helpful to women like me. But I had been told that this wouldn't be possible for a few years because of that institution's security policies. It seemed unlikely that I'd ever be able to go back sober to the place I returned to so many times while drinking.

And yet now, with the help of video technology, I was about to do just that. The cameraman told me where to stand. He turned the lights on and all of a sudden I was looking at the familiar housing unit in the prison 200 miles away. I saw tables lined with women who were scheduled for release, just as I had been so many times. I recognized some of them from my time there.

I shared about going to AA in the very same prison where they now sat. I told them how they too could begin attending meetings before they even left. I shared how I learned that recovery was an inside job and how through AA I had found a new freedom while still in prison.

I also shared about all the times I'd made plans before the prison gates were opened and how I never followed through on those plans until I went to AA, which was where I learned to act right.

Before AA, I had big ideas about how to live on the outside. I'd wanted to stay sober, but I hadn't been able to without AA. I told them what it had been like this time getting out—my mom was dead, my son didn't even know me—but I'd stayed sober. It worked for me and it could work for them.

As I spoke, I saw guards bending down to look at the screen. Some of them I recognized. These corrections professionals usually saw the worst of me, but on this day, because of technology, they got to see the best of me.

Tracy B.
St. Louis, Missouri

In a Canberra Jail
August 2020

This was a horrible mistake. I was seated in a small white room. Two steel chairs were bolted to the floor with a steel table, also bolted to the floor between them. I sat across the table from a man who was dressed in a prison jumpsuit. We obviously had nothing in common. What could I say to him? We stared at each other in silence while I pondered how I had gotten myself into this mess.

I had arrived in Canberra, Australia from Toronto a couple of months earlier. I was three years sober and the Promises had been coming true. The fire department where I worked had wanted to get rid of me three years earlier. But I was sober now. Things were different. They selected me for a professional exchange with the Australian Capital Territory Fire Brigade. I arrived in Canberra brimming with confidence.

Things started well at my new fire station. I had a nice place to live in a trendy part of town. I was enjoying the great Aussie outdoors. I was hiking, sailing, even playing a little rugby and cricket. I did all the things my sponsor, Tim, and other AA friends back home had suggested. I got a local temporary sponsor named Arthur. I joined a group and went to lots of other meetings. I kept up my routine of AA reading and daily meditation.

But something was off. After a couple of months, I became restless and irritable. It would pass, I told myself. Perhaps it was a touch of homesickness. Or maybe I was finally coming down off that pink cloud. I tried to ignore the feeling, but some of my character defects started to rear their ugly heads, such as a tendency to isolate and judge others, as well as my habit of telling people, "I'm fine."

When I tired of wallowing in my own misery, I picked up the phone and called Tim back in Toronto and told him how I was feeling.

"Sounds like you need to get active. Find some service work," Tim told me. "You're in a wonderful situation. Most people would love to have the opportunity you do. Stop feeling sorry for yourself and find someone to help. Ask Arthur what's available."

Tim was big on service. He had started me off emptying ash trays. I'd moved on to coffee service, then group librarian and Intergroup representative. All the safe and cozy jobs.

Tim was active in corrections. Ever since I had reached the required one-year mark he had asked me to join him. He said there was a chronic need for volunteers to bring AA meetings to local jails. I kept putting him off. I had lots of excuses. The biggest one was that I had never done any time. I had somehow managed to tiptoe through the minefield, without even doing an overnighter. Beneath all the excuses, though, was fear.

On Tim's advice, I asked Arthur what service opportunities were available. I was thinking maybe a half-year commitment to a newcomers' meeting, or maybe a spot on the organizing committee for a local roundup.

"Well, we always need help with the jail," Arthur told me. I was flabbergasted. I angrily accused Arthur of conspiring behind my back with Tim back home. I later made amends for my outburst and we laughed about it, but at the time I was really mad. I stewed about the situation for a couple of days and came up with what I thought was a brilliant idea: I would show them what an utter disaster I would be.

So I joined the Canberra AA Corrections team. I passed the police check and a date was made for my first jail visit. In Canberra in the 90s jail meetings were done one-on-one.

That was how I came to be sitting in that small room across the table from this Aboriginal man. He was giving me a curious grin. I knew nothing about him or what he had done. We were from completely opposite sides of the planet: geographically, socially, economically and just about every other way you could imagine. I grew up in middle-class comfort in Canada. I was given tons of opportunities, most of which I had squandered. He knew nothing about hockey. I knew nothing about life in the Outback.

So we sat in silence and looked at each other. I didn't know at the time that in Aboriginal culture, silence was a sign of wisdom. I didn't feel wise. I felt like an idiot, fear creeping up the back of my neck like a lizard. The silence seemed to go on forever. In reality, it was probably only 20 or 30 seconds.

When I couldn't take it anymore, I blurted out, "You know how when you wake up in the morning and you're so sick and so full of guilt and shame for the crap you did the night before that the only thing you can possibly do is grab the bottle and start drinking again until the fog settles in and it just doesn't matter anymore? And then you do it all over again." I was gripping the edges of the cold steel table so hard my knuckles were white.

The man's grin blossomed into a full-fledged smile and he nodded enthusiastically. "Ya mate, I know exactly what you're talkin' about there" he said. "My name's Jim."

Suddenly all my fear melted away, all the differences I had imagined between us. We were simply one alcoholic talking with another. The rest of our hour together flew by. Jim and I shared bits of our stories. I did my best to hold out the lifeline of hope. I told him there was a program of practical action in the Twelve Steps of AA. I told him the cycle of alcoholism could be broken and lives rebuilt, if he was willing to do the work.

When we were done, I walked out of that jail with a mixture of exhilaration and humility. I felt whole, useful and connected to the world and its people in a way I had never experienced before.

I don't know what happened to Jim. I hope a seed was planted, but I'll never know. That's good for me. You see, I'm the kind of guy who likes to turn to the last page to see how the story ends. I can't do that in jail. I've spoken in federal prisons but mostly I work in local jails, so I rarely see an inmate for longer than a few months. I need to leave the results in the hands of a Higher Power, way beyond my understanding.

I've been taking AA into jails for over 20 years now. Sometimes the meetings are just a bunch of guys trying to pass the time. That's fine. I had no desire to stop drinking at my first AA meeting either. But sometimes there's a guy like Marcel, who for the first time since he was a kid got six months sober in jail. He asked me to pick up a six-month chip for him, even though he knew I wouldn't be able to give it to him. We're not allowed to bring in hard plastic or metal, anything that could be made into a weapon. Marcel wanted me to pick up that chip anyway and tell my home group that he was sober for six months and full of gratitude. I still have that chip. Those are the experiences that give me goosebumps.

As a firefighter, I had to be prepared to rush into burning buildings, but I had been afraid to take the AA message into jail. Now I can't imagine not doing corrections work. What I had really been afraid of was being emotionally open and vulnerable. I had felt different all my life and I built a wall, thick and strong, to protect myself. The first real crack in that wall was made sitting in that small white room with that man in the Canberra jail.

I hope I said something that helped Jim. He gave me more than he could ever imagine.

John K.
Carleton Place, Ontario

Maximum Picnic

July 2018

Six years ago, I found myself in the parking lot outside of what would be my first AA meeting. Just released from jail, I was terrified and angry. Why had I listened to that guy from the AA helpline? I didn't want to be here. I may have just been released from jail, but I felt sure my life wasn't that unmanageable. Or was it?

I'd rather be dead than go into the meeting, but I had reached a state of hopelessness that I never imagined I would sink to. And yet, with a gentle shove from God, I moved slowly toward the door. I saw a man standing in the entrance with his back turned to me. I approached him and asked if this was AA. He turned around and gave me a big smile. "Yes, it is," he said. "I am so glad you made it here. We've been waiting for you."

So, full of shame and guilt, I walked down those stairs and took a seat. I was amazed at how many people were there. With the ring of a bell, the man who greeted me at the door began to speak. The room fell silent. I don't remember much about what was said, but I do remember the topic of discussion. It was Step One.

Looking back now, I feel God had handpicked each member there that night. I heard myself in every one of those members who shared their stories. I knew I was in the right place. I was home.

Just two nights earlier, I had woken up in a different jail cell. I had sworn it would never happen again, yet there I was again. And this time it was the worst. I called out to God. It was the first time I earnestly did that. I truly believe he answered my desperate plea.

Covered in blood, without my shoes and still in my pajamas from a few days earlier, I was confused and full of remorse and dread. I was taken from my cell, after sleeping off the worst of it, and led down a seemingly endless hallway where I was fingerprinted and photographed.

I began to remember small bits of what had happened. My stomach sank as I recalled my son's screams for help after I wrecked my car. Fortunately, the impact had been on my side. I found my car wrapped around a utility pole. If things had gone differently, I could have killed my son. For me, the end had arrived. Either I got help or I died.

Hours passed. I was finally released with a promise to appear in court. I was now facing serious charges and if I were convicted, I could serve many years behind bars. Truth was, I already felt like I was in a kind of prison.

Someone then put me in the back seat of a taxicab, still without shoes, covered in blood and not knowing where my son was. To be honest, I never even asked. I was driven home, jail papers in hand, where I would break into my parents' house, steal more of their money to pay the cab driver, and invite him in for a drink. He swiftly declined the offer and I slammed the door in his face.

I knew a drink would make it all disappear. Even after my plea to God and my desperate call for help, I still wanted a drink. Then oblivion came.

The following day, I made a call to AA, a call that would forever change my life. I have remained sober ever since. AA showed me that what I thought was impossible—a life without booze—was possible.

After I'd been sober about four months, I was approached by a member to attend a meeting at a prison. I thought it was a joke at first. I had been locked up in that very prison. I never thought I'd ever go back there, especially for an AA meeting! Reluctantly, I agreed. AA had never said no to me, so how could I say no to AA?

That Friday night, I sat with incarcerated AA members for the very first time. I was still new then, still angry and full of fear. Then a member said, "Ruth, why don't you share how you have stayed sober." That prison meeting was a life-changing experience for me. I saw myself in every member sitting there. I could have easily been any one of them. From that moment on, attending prison meetings has remained a privilege and an honor. We have all done bad things; that doesn't make us bad people. Today, some of my favorite people call prison their home.

Not long ago, I was invited to attend an AA picnic at a "supermax" prison in upstate New York. I had visited this institution a few times before and was grateful to be invited to join our friends for this annual event. But I had no idea what a prison picnic would be like.

When we arrived at the facility, we were escorted by guards and began the long walk down the empty hallways, stopping frequently for more security checks. Passing the separated yards through the heavily barred windows, I caught a small glimpse of the lives lived there. Shivers went up my spine. I felt overwhelmed as my eyes began to fill. I had a giant lump in my throat. I got to see for the first time how these men live every single day. Endless towering concrete walls as high as the sky, razor wire and fences everywhere. Guards everywhere. I was deafened by the silence. It was like entering another world. I was sad, yet happy and excited. I was feeling so many things all at once that I thought I'd burst. In that moment, I paused and reached out to God.

When we finally reached our yard, we were led by the guards and filed in one by one. Word was sent out to another group of guards to send in the inmates. The outside AA members had arrived.

The sober inmates had been busy preparing for this day. A group of picnic tables had been assembled under a giant canopy to shelter us from the sun. Tables for food were set up and ready. There was even a DJ table for music. But where are the guys? I thought. Why is it taking so long? Then, out of the corner of my eye I saw a shadow. I turned quickly to see who was there but whatever had been there was gone. I looked across the yard and goose bumps covered my body. I felt the presence of God. I took a silent moment and asked him to bring us all together.

Just then, the men walked into the yard. The sun was shining and they were all smiling. The joy and freedom I saw in their eyes was magical. With a silent nod and warm handshake, we all stood together. For a moment, it seemed we all forgot where we were. The razor wire disappeared; the giant walls no longer seemed so towering. We talked one-to-one and in small groups. Like at any other meeting, we shared together, caught up and then made our way to the canopy.

The AA meeting in the yard was about to begin. I began to cry.

The prisoners led the AA meeting. I was filled with such gratitude listening to our friends share. It was something I will never forget.

In the yard of a supermax prison, I heard hope, I saw love and I felt at home. It was amazing. I witnessed as grown men cried and laughed together. These men were my friends.

Since the picnic was an annual gathering, we were given much more time with the guys. We sat and had lunch that the sober inmates had prepared for us. Afterward, we listened to music and talked and talked. The day gave me so much joy. It was like nothing I have ever experienced.

As members of AA, we are given such amazing opportunities to serve. I now know what it means to be of maximum service to the Fellowship that saved my life.

When the picnic ended, we were allowed to gather together for a group photo, for those who wished to join. On the count of three, several pictures were taken, one of which now sits in a frame on my bedside table as a lasting memory. I keep it close to my heart. Every day, I wake up to my beautiful friends' faces and give thanks to AA and God.

Ruth L.
Beaconsfield, Quebec

I Didn't Want to Go to Prison

February 1985

For a little more than a quarter of a century, I have been attending AA meetings in correctional institutions on a weekly basis. The majority of those meetings were evenly divided between a county workhouse and a maximum security state prison, which gave me two such meetings per week over most of that time.

Why?

In the first place, it wasn't exactly my idea. When I started to become active in AA, my sponsor told me to do whatever was suggested and ask questions afterward. So when I was asked to speak at a jail or in the state prison, I did.

But I didn't like it. I got a nasty feeling in my spine every time that door or gate clanged or clicked shut behind me. The only time it felt good was when I left. I also thought that those on the inside couldn't identify with my white-collar drinking story, rough as it was. I had never done time, and I felt that they looked on me as some sort of snobbish do-gooder.

Then one evening, after about four years in the program, I was driving home from a meeting at a state mental hospital and thanking my Higher Power that that was over, when a voice spoke to me clearly, saying: "From now on, your principal work in AA will be in correctional institutions!"

My reflex answer was: "The hell you say!" It was the last thing I wanted to do. I liked jails and prisons even less than mental hospitals.

But I had learned to do what I was told in AA, and this sounded a lot like my Higher Power telling me what to do. It certainly wasn't my idea. So I went to the warden of the local workhouse and arranged with him to set up a meeting there. One of the conditions he made was that I be personally responsible for every meeting—which meant I had to be there every week.

A short time later, I was scheduled to speak at the state prison. At that point, I had been fingerprinted and cleared as part of a very limited list of eligible speakers. The night I was due, I felt like calling someone else on the list and offering to swap dates. I was dog-tired and felt as if I were coming down with a cold, and there was a fight I wanted to watch on TV. But I went anyway, mentally kicking myself for having gotten involved in the first place, and oozing resentment all the way to the meeting.

I can't tell you what I said that night or what took place during the discussion that followed. All I remember is that I left that meeting feeling like a million dollars. My incipient cold had vanished. I was no longer tired. I had forgotten about the TV fight. The next day, I called the group sponsor and asked if he needed help. He did.

From then on, I started to attend meetings in the prison every week.

Working in correctional institutions has helped me in a number of ways—all of them spiritual (an area in which I needed, and still need, a great deal of help). One of my principal character defects has always been lying, or stretching the truth. Before writing down my Fourth Step, I had to take it aloud in front of a mirror in order to curb this tendency.

Anyone who has worked for any length of time in a correctional institution group will tell you that you can't lie to the inmates! In the first place, you feel a moral obligation to be honest with them, and that helps. But the real truth is, they can spot a phony every time, and they can ask some very searching questions. I have learned a lot about myself by having to answer their questions honestly. I found that I had to look at myself in a new light—a much brighter one than I had been accustomed to using. I was often uncomfortable, but I always benefited.

In addition, I have an ego problem. This can play havoc with an AA member like me, since I am articulate and, as a result, have been a speaker on the "convention circuit." Don't let anyone tell you that it isn't an ego trip when you are met at the airport, driven to a fancy hotel where you get a deluxe room and VIP treatment, and then get up to speak to an audience of anywhere from several hundred to a thousand or more.

It always serves to bring me back to earth when, the following Tuesday, I find myself back with my small group of inmates. Other people are doing the speaking, and I realize that I am there only because I am a drunk who is staying sober one day at a time, and that my constant presence at meetings is merely a small, but a continuing, indication that the program of AA works.

Periodically, newcomers or non-AAs ask me, in all innocence, "But don't you get bored going to meetings after 30 years?"

I tell them no, but I seldom bother to explain one of the reasons for my lack of boredom. In my prison group, there are always new members. The speakers are often individuals whom I have heard many,

many times. I could tell you their detailed case histories—in some cases, almost word for word. But when they speak in that room in the prison, I do not listen to them with my own ears. I listen with the ears of the new member! In this way, my old friends sound fresh and inspiring each time they speak, and I find myself discovering things I had never heard before in their talks.

I have only one serious problem with correctional institution meetings. What can I possibly do to give my friends the inmates one-tenth of the help that they have given me over the years, and still keep giving me every week?

Anonymous
Metuchen, New Jersey

The Walls Will Come Down
July 2013

My drinking brought me many fears, but the worst fear of all was that someday I would get locked up in prison because of my actions in a drunken blackout. Therefore, I stayed isolated from the rest of the world in the last two years of my active alcoholic paranoia. In doing so, I had created my own prison of fear—quite a paradox.

Eventually, I found my way to AA as a result of the desperation of these accumulating fears. After about 14 months of sobriety, that desperation returned with a vengeance: I was not drinking, but that's all. I had become my own sponsor and had done some of the Steps in my head. The results were obvious because of the conflict still inside of me. I was certainly not happy, joyous and free like some others seemed to be. But pride needed to take a backseat because I was dying inside. So I finally asked a man to be my sponsor, and he walked me through the Steps in the Big Book. A sense of well-being began to enter into my life.

He was professionally involved in the prison system and he introduced me to a new "Bridges" program. This kind of service consisted of outside AA members meeting with inside members at their "sober houses" in a minimum-security prison and discussing the first three Steps around their kitchen table. I can't begin to tell you the mixed emotions I was feeling at the time. But one day, on a memorable drive home from doing this service, I realized that God had freed me from one of my most prominent fears. I was transformed in what I can only describe now as some sort of spiritual experience.

Since that time, I have had the privilege of attending many prison facilities in this region as an outside AA member. I have had the honor of personally escorting inmates to many outside AA meetings or functions, and I've become a temporary sponsor when they're released or at halfway houses. I also write to others through the Corrections Correspondence program available through our General Service Office. Currently, we're reading the Big Book with a small group of inside members and a few dedicated ones outside.

God has truly blessed my life in the place that I had once dreaded the most. My best thinking could not have possibly come close to this as a solution to the many problems that I had in my life. God led me to this Fellowship and, in doing so, allowed me to meet the people I needed to find the courage necessary to overcome my overwhelming fears.

None of the many wonderful experiences I have been blessed with in the past years have touched me as much as one I just recently had. It began when we tried restarting an AA group inside a maximum-security prison in the north of the province. They had not had a meeting in well over three years at that facility. Some people told us it would be a waste of time. Besides, what would be the point? It would not work for any length of time. My first sponsor just smiled and commented that when God wants it, walls will come down. With the encouragement and help of a few dedicated AA members and an interest from certain corrections staff at the prison, it's been going strong for the past two years now. Once a month we put on two meetings, one after the other for the different units.

One inside member, I'll call him Jake, had been coming right from the beginning. He's a solid man and a descendant of the Maliseet people. He had a big smile every time we met. He always seemed to have a new guy in tow with him at most meetings.

Early last year, Jake was not showing up at the meetings anymore, which seemed odd to me. I asked the programs officer if he had been transferred. She said he was in segregation—"the hole"—due to an internal conflict of some sort and could not attend the meetings any longer.

The programs officer was clearly disappointed because she knew how much AA seemed to help him. A few more months passed, and still there was no sign of Jake. The programmer asked later if it would be possible for one of us to have a one-on-one meeting with Jake in segregation. The following month we showed up and she asked if we were still willing to go into the hole since the warden had approved it.

When I arrived at the guard station in segregation many of the corrections officers seemed to be perplexed at my being there. They asked if Jake would need shackles? I told them that I didn't think they were necessary. When Jake showed up, he raised his arms and wiggled his large hands as a sign of freedom. With his broad smile he was saying, "No chains." Apparently, anytime they are brought out of their cell in the hole they are almost always shackled. We talked as long as possible, and I was permitted to pass him a few Grapevines, which he really enjoyed reading, especially in his new living quarters.

On the way back to the regular meeting I asked the programmer if this type of privilege happened often, since the guards seemed to be a bit mystified. She smiled and said it was a first for her. Later, I asked my first sponsor, who was knowledgeable about corrections affairs, and he said he had never heard of a regular AA member ever being allowed in the hole in that facility. He also reminded me again that when God wants it to happen, the walls will come down. At this time I was humbled by just how powerful AA is, and I started to respect this genuine gift from God. The privileges that have come to me because of this new way of life have gone far beyond what I could have ever imagined.

Just recently, Jake was moved to a medium-security prison, which we visit more regularly. He was at the AA meeting the other day, and he arrived with a huge smile and a newcomer in tow. He's doing what we have been trying to do all along: carrying the message of freedom inside the walls. I too can safely say that I have found my freedom in—of all places—a prison.

Dave A.
Moncton, New Brunswick

They Wait For Us
July 2016

I currently serve as the Recording Secretary for Area 56. My sobriety date is July 25, 1982 and my home group is the Complete Abandon Group that meets Tuesdays at noon in Kettering, Ohio. If you're ever in the neighborhood, please drop in. We're a small, friendly Big Book study.

For many years, I resisted service and told myself that it was for newcomers, to help them get sober. It took me a long time to look at myself, but I finally learned in AA to be responsible when anyone, anywhere reaches out for help.

About 10 months ago, I went to a Twelfth Step workshop in the Dayton Correctional Institution (DCI), a prison that houses female inmates. I said that I'd be interested in helping start AA meetings there. I didn't know what to expect, but I showed up. After much debate, we decided on a format. It's like a beginners' meeting; there's a different chairperson each month, and we choose topics from AA literature.

Perhaps not surprisingly, a number of addict/alcoholics also attend the meeting. It's important to gently but firmly direct attention toward our only requirement for AA membership—a desire to stop drinking. That helps improve focus in the meeting, but it takes patience and persistence. There is still a lot of confusion about the difference between NA and AA, and we try to make it as simple as possible, while sticking to AA's singleness of purpose.

It's important to remember that we aren't missionaries or therapists or group facilitators; we're alcoholics just like the women who wait for us to show up, week after week. I once sat next to a young woman who didn't look like she could be any older than 22 or so. She spoke up to say that she had served 13 years before her first parole hearing. I was shocked. I decided that if she was stuck in here for 13 years, the least I could do is show up for this AA meeting once a week.

These women wait for us to arrive. If one of us isn't there, the women ask about her. It matters. And it matters to me that I know that they wait for us. The phenomenon of "waiting for someone to arrive" is an important part of that special connection to AA. And not just for inmates. It was important for me early on, and it still is. There are people at my meetings who I look forward to seeing each week, people I know I can count on. It makes AA feel like home.

Many of these women have been sober before on the outside, sometimes for as long as five, 10 or 15 years. Many of them, for one reason or another, lost their connection to AA and started drinking again. Their drinking led them to prison. That woke me up. The women bring an important experience to our meetings. So many are disappointed with themselves. At the meeting, we try to stress a day at a time and offer each other comfort, while talking program every chance we get.

A couple of weeks ago, one of the women asked me, "What do you do when you're stuck in self-pity?" It was a real watershed moment for me, because it was so heartfelt, so perfectly AA. I shared with her that my number one antidote is my gratitude list. It was strange telling an inmate to list the things she could be grateful for, but I tried to come up with a few right off the bat. I learned how to do this from other women who got tired of my self-pity and my love affair with it. Today I get to pass this experience on.

Our Monday DCI meeting continually reminds me that I have sober experience to share and that I always have more to learn. It also shows me what can happen if I don't stay attached to AA and make it a vital part of my life. These women provide me with living, breathing examples of people who have a desperate desire to get sober and stay sober. They are my peers. I get to be with women who want a way up and out of this disease. We get to share love and a depth of feeling I have only ever known in Alcoholics Anonymous. I want us to give them hope, because hope was given to me. I was once sad and broken too.

Our Big Book has a wonderful passage about usefulness:

"Those of us who have spent much time in the world of spiritual make-believe have eventually seen the childishness of it. This dream world has been replaced by a great sense of purpose, accompanied by a growing consciousness of the power of God in our lives. We have come to believe he would like us to keep our heads in the clouds with him, but that our feet ought to be firmly planted on earth. That is where our fellow travelers are, and that is where our work must be done. These are the realities for us. We have found nothing incompatible between a powerful spiritual experience and a life of sane and happy usefulness."

Every week, in that prison, I get to be reminded that freedom from the bondage of self and the freedom to be useful is the greatest freedom of all.

Laura G.
Miamisburg, Ohio

Better Than Monday Night Football

July 2019

A couple of years ago, my sponsor suggested I look into trying to carry the message into our local jail. I talked to a few old-timers in the area and they all said it would be a waste of time; that the jail hadn't allowed AA inside in quite a few years.

I told my sponsor of these obstacles and he said, "If you truly want to help people, God won't make it too hard."

He gave me directions on how to go about making contact with the director of the jail. I had planned to just send the director an email, but my sponsor suggested I follow up the email with a phone call to ask to meet with him.

So I followed my sponsor's suggestions and met with the director. He thought an AA meeting in the jail was a great idea and told me to get back to him with details on when I wanted to start.

I went back to my home group and asked if anyone else was interested. Quite a few members volunteered, and we decided to take a meeting into the jail on Monday nights. We carried our first AA meeting into a local county detention center and it was a big hit. But as time went on, the number of volunteers we had for the meeting began to drop. I was beginning to become disheartened.

Then, one Monday night, we went into the "pod" and an inmate there said that it was a sign from God that AA had shown up. He shared how he was supposed to have gone to an AA roundup that weekend, but instead he and his girlfriend had decided to get a 30-pack of beer and go over to the river. He ended up in jail, and the story of his arrest made it onto the local news. His girlfriend ended up in the hospital in a coma.

At the end of our meeting, this man and I talked. I shared with him about the Twelve Steps and about the Big Book. I gave him a card with my number on it and told him we'd be back to see him.

As fate would have it, when we went back the following Monday the jail was on lockdown. This happened week after week. We would show up for the meeting only to be turned away at the door due to the lockdown. This took its toll on my desire to serve because I had taken time away from my family, and the lockdown meant I did not even get to carry the message inside.

One Monday night, following all the canceled meetings due to the lockdown, I was driving to the jail and my thoughts were running a million miles per second. I thought of all the volunteers who had stopped coming and who were still sober. I thought of all the members who never volunteered and who were still sober. At that moment,

I thought about the fact that I could have been be at home with my wife and daughters, watching Monday Night Football. Thankfully, my feet had been trained by AA and the next thing I knew, I was getting out of my car at the jail, giving Mark (the other member who carries the jail meeting with me) a hug.

We said a quick prayer and pressed the buzzer for the intercom. Finally, the guards opened the doors for us. How many drunks are grateful to be allowed into jail? I don't know the answer, but I know I sure was.

As we walked into the pod, I saw a familiar face. I couldn't recall his name, but knew he had attended one of our meetings in the past. I walked up to him, offered my hand, and said, "I believe you were here the last time we came. It's been about two months." He looked at me with tears in his eyes. He said, "It's been 71 days." It was the man who drank the 30-pack with his girlfriend by the river and ended up in jail.

Out of his pocket, he pulled the card I had given him 71 days before. He said, "I slept with your card in my pocket for the first month after you gave it to me. It made me feel safe. I got one of the Big Books from the library and I've started reading it. When you came the day after I had arrived here, I knew for the first time in a long time that everything was going to be OK. I knew this because you guys had shown up."

I left the jail that night with tears in my eyes and a new gratitude for AA and the men and women who day after day, year after year, continue to "suit up and show up."

I was so close to giving up on the jail meeting, but thanks to God, the Twelve Steps and great sponsorship, I followed my feet instead of my thoughts.

When I needed help, when I was hopeless, the hand of AA reached out to me. Today, I have the responsibility and privilege of giving it back.

Bill B.
Tahlequah, Oklahoma

The Twelve Steps

1. We admitted we were powerless over alcohol—that our lives had become unmanageable.
2. Came to believe that a Power greater than ourselves could restore us to sanity.
3. Made a decision to turn our will and our lives over to the care of God *as we understood Him*.
4. Made a searching and fearless moral inventory of ourselves.
5. Admitted to God, to ourselves, and to another human being the exact nature of our wrongs.
6. Were entirely ready to have God remove all these defects of character.
7. Humbly asked Him to remove our shortcomings.
8. Made a list of all persons we had harmed, and became willing to make amends to them all.
9. Made direct amends to such people wherever possible, except when to do so would injure them or others.
10. Continued to take personal inventory and when we were wrong promptly admitted it.
11. Sought through prayer and meditation to improve our conscious contact with God *as we understood Him*, praying only for knowledge of His will for us and the power to carry that out.
12. Having had a spiritual awakening as the result of these steps, we tried to carry this message to alcoholics, and to practice these principles in all our affairs.

The Twelve Traditions

1. Our common welfare should come first; personal recovery depends upon A.A. unity.
2. For our group purpose there is but one ultimate authority—a loving God as He may express Himself in our group conscience. Our leaders are but trusted servants; they do not govern.
3. The only requirement for A.A. membership is a desire to stop drinking.
4. Each group should be autonomous except in matters affecting other groups or A.A. as a whole.
5. Each group has but one primary purpose—to carry its message to the alcoholic who still suffers.
6. An A.A. group ought never endorse, finance or lend the A.A. name to any related facility or outside enterprise, lest problems of money, property and prestige divert us from our primary purpose.
7. Every A.A. group ought to be fully self-supporting, declining outside contributions.
8. Alcoholics Anonymous should remain forever nonprofessional, but our service centers may employ special workers.
9. A.A., as such, ought never be organized; but we may create service boards or committees directly responsible to those they serve.
10. Alcoholics Anonymous has no opinion on outside issues; hence the A.A. name ought never be drawn into public controversy.
11. Our public relations policy is based on attraction rather than promotion; we need always maintain personal anonymity at the level of press, radio and films.
12. Anonymity is the spiritual foundation of all our traditions, ever reminding us to place principles before personalities.

AA Grapevine

AA Grapevine is AA's international monthly journal, published continuously since its first issue in June 1944. The AA pamphlet on AA Grapevine describes its scope and purpose this way: "As an integral part of Alcoholics Anonymous since 1944, the Grapevine publishes articles that reflect the full diversity of experience and thought found within the A.A. Fellowship, as does La Viña, the bimonthly Spanish-language magazine, first published in 1996. No one viewpoint or philosophy dominates their pages, and in determining content, the editorial staff relies on the principles of the Twelve Traditions."

In addition to magazines, AA Grapevine, Inc. also produces books, eBooks, audiobooks and other items. It also offers a Grapevine Complete subscription, which includes the print magazine as well as complete online access, with new stories weekly, AudioGrapevine (the audio version of the magazine), the vast Grapevine Story Archive and current online issues of Grapevine and La Viña. A separate ePub version of the magazines are also available. For more information on AA Grapevine, or to subscribe to any of these, please visit the magazine's website at aagrapevine.org or write to:

AA Grapevine, Inc.
475 Riverside Drive
New York, NY 10115

Alcoholics Anonymous

AA's program of recovery is fully set forth in its basic text, *Alcoholics Anonymous* (commonly known as the Big Book), now in its Fourth Edition, as well as in *Twelve Steps and Twelve Traditions, Living Sober,* and other books. Information on AA can also be found on AA's website at www.aa.org, or by writing to:

Alcoholics Anonymous
Box 459
Grand Central Station
New York, NY 10163

For local resources, check your local telephone directory under "Alcoholics Anonymous." Four pamphlets, "This is A.A.," "Is A.A. For You?," "44 Questions," and "A Newcomer Asks" are also available from AA.